"What an insightful and inspirational read! After many years of performing, teaching and directing dance, it's wonderful to read this book about comparing the process of building a solid foundation for dance technique to building a solid foundation for business. Patricia Vaccarino has hit the mark by expressing the importance of taking baby steps, of having commitment and paying attention to details to achieve the big picture goal."

— Julie Tobiason, Dancer, Seattle Dance Project,
former Principal Dancer PNB, Ballet Instructor PNB

"Steps is full of charming, insightful and lighthearted comparisons between ballet and business that are totally relevant for anyone who is intent on exploring excellence."

— Alexandra Dickson, Dancer, Seattle Dance Project,
former soloist PNB, Ballet and Pilates Instructor

"Patricia Vaccarino's book is beautiful, like a conversation with an old friend, straightforward and inspiring. Vaccarino has done her research and collected an extensive compendium of dance references from ballerinas, choreographers, and teachers. Like Jonathan Raban's mode of incorporating literary and historical references into his narratives, Vaccarino weaves the dancers' words into her narrative, always with the purpose of instilling her message, to encourage and inspire anyone pursuing an endeavor to undertake the hard work, see the incremental progress, embrace corrections, and ultimately find fulfillment in one's effort."

— Mary Englund, Seattle Attorney, Hobbyist Dancer

"In Steps, Patricia is showing us how to receive a bounty through honest action… A close examination of this book reveals the depth of knowledge she has of process and the passionate generosity integral to making each step create results."

— Annie de Vuono, Dance Instructor, eXitSPACE studio, Milliner, Owner de Vuono Hats

"The title of Patricia Vaccarino's new book is an effective metaphor. There are the stair steps up in her grandmother's house, which she mastered decades ago; there are the steps of a ballet class—the central metaphor of the book. Also, the steps of growing a business and a brand—the subject of the book. "Steps" is more than a business manual; it is part memoir, part meditation on the inner world of the ballet class, part exhortation to excellence: a paean to stretching beyond one's reach. Dance is her vision quest, the focus of her drive to experience the fullness of the moment—dance, she says, is what God watches. And from that experience, she draws a series of metaphors for life, and business as a natural extension."

— Manny Frishberg, Journalist

"As a professional dancer and teacher I not only teach dance but also instill qualities such as discipline, commitment and perseverance. It was enlightening to read such a candid adult student perspective and see how inspired dance lessons can lead to success in any business."

— Timothy Lynch, Co-artistic Director, Dancer, Seattle Dance Project, Dance Educator, Ballet Instructor PNB

pr for people® Steps

Patricia Vaccarino

pr for people®
Steps

Ballet + Business = Brand Philosophy

My not-so-secret life as an
adult dancer and how it impacts
my life and business.

Patricia Vaccarino

Xanthus Publishing • Seattle, WA

Copyright © 2017, 2011 by Patricia Vaccarino
All rights reserved, including the right to reproduce this book or portions thereof in any form whatsoever.

For information, address:
Xanthus Publishing
2212 Queen Anne Avenue North, PMB 615
Seattle, WA 98109

Originally published in 2012 by Cedar Forge Press
ISBN 978-1-936672-21-9

19 18 17   2 3 4 5

ISBN 978-0-9963494-3-7
Library of Congress Control Number: 2017917099
Printed in the U.S.A.

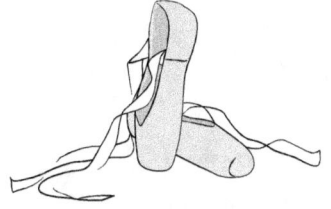

Dedicated to my husband,
Joseph M. Puggelli,

and to my three children:
David, Katie and Sarah

Table of Contents

These chapters are named for the core principles I have encountered in every dance class. It did not matter if the class was large or small, located in a rural area or at a prestigious dance school in New York City. It did not matter if the teacher had achieved fame in the dance world. Certain truths prevailed and entered my body, making me see connections and patterns that had little to do with dance and everything to do with life.

Introduction 1

1. First Steps 5

2. Positioning 19

3. Small Adjustments 31

4. The Four Corners of the Room 49

5. Rising Higher 69

6. Balance 89

7. Fall and Recovery 105

8. Hitting Your Marks 129

Acknowledgments

In special gratitude for my teachers, who gave me instruction in ballet, modern dance, Pilates, technique, and life: Marisa Albee, Kari Anderson, Robert Atwood, Elaine Bauer, Peter Boal, Elaine Bonow, Stephanie Cain, Jennifer Carroll, Michele Golden Curtis, Annie de Vuono, Alexandra Dickson, Jocelyn Edelstein, Emilietta Ettlin, Paul Gibson, Oleg Gorboulev, Gelsey Kirkland, Dana Hanson, David Howard, Timothy Lynch, Stanko Milov, Anton Pankevich, Jocelyn Paoli, Meg Potter, Pamela Probisco, Zena Rommett, Sarah Shira, Jeff Stanton, Kathryn Sullivan, Marjorie Thompson, Julie Tobiason, Bruce Wells, Marguerite Wesley, Le Yin, and "Tatiana."

Special thanks to the studios where I have taken classes in Seattle and New York:

Belltown Ballet
eXitSPACE studio
Pacific Northwest Ballet (PNB)
Pro-Robics
Steps on Broadway
Westside Dance Project

In respect and admiration for Seattle Dance Project, a world-class dance company composed of gifted dancers, many of whom have been my instructors.

A heartfelt thanks to my first ballet teacher, Annie de Vuono.

Special thanks to my editors, Linda Jay Geldens and Fred Strong. Together, we made many small adjustments!

pr for people® Steps

Patricia Vaccarino

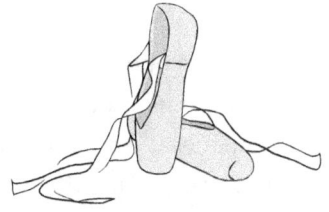

Introduction

Steps is a business book, but it is more than an ordinary business book. Although it encompasses the concept of business + dance = brand philosophy, the term *branding* is rarely mentioned. ***Steps*** is about dance and business as much as it is about life. On a higher level of thinking, all of these elements are interrelated. The connections you learn about your body in dance inspire you to see the connections in all things. ***Steps*** means you must climb the same steps many times before there is any wisdom to be found. The true process of stair-stepping is about tearing down, reconfiguring and rebuilding one's soul. In ***Steps***, I am suggesting that you should not even consider building a brand unless you are willing to do very hard work, the same way a dancer learns technique, movement and artistry through very hard work. You can't build a brand unless you are willing to explore excellence.

Steps is about my not-so-secret life as an adult dancer and how I move every day. While I train consistently in ballet, every so often I step out of ballet into another form of dance: fusion, zumba, hip-hop or modern. Sometimes I call other forms of dance *the anti-ballet*, because of their rambling freedom, gyrations, and chaos. Every time I walk through the subway shuttle underpass in Grand Central Station, I see *homies* doing hip-hop, and I want to step out and dance with them. Any form of dance is, to me, a celebration of life. Even when I'm not in the studio, I am dancing in my head.

Through hard work and devotion, I have come to know that dance is a great metaphor for life and for business. In my world view, I equate life with business. And good business practices are as essential to your life as every breath you take. Good business means you are performing well—to the best of your ability, whether anyone is watching you or not. What matters is that you do your absolute best to hit your own marks.

Steps are the building blocks of dance, but the name *Steps* was inspired from a childhood home, an old tenement in Yonkers, New York. *Steps* was also inspired by the dance school *Steps on Broadway* in New York City. Every time I traveled to New York on business, I took classes at Steps. New York is home for me, and certainly home for the dance world.

During my journey as an adult dancer in the past five years, I have come to learn more about dance than I ever thought possible. I am simply a woman who one day started to train in dance. Ever since then, I have not wanted to stop. And why should I ever want to stop? When you dance, you are young at heart, your body is nimble and quick, and you feel that you will live forever. In some ways, you will live forever.

Every day we take first steps. First steps might impact your life for a day, a week, a month or years to come. Those first steps may be on the road to recovery, in a twelve-step program for AA, embarking on a new career, going into or out of a relationship, starting up a new business or building an existing business or maintaining a growing business. Whether our first steps are physical or metaphorical, the process itself is action-oriented and always difficult, but it is the most rewarding thing you will ever do.

Steps can be special and mysterious, taking on a metaphorical quality as they become a powerful way to define the truth.

The concept of "taking one's first step" is often overrated. After taking a first step, no one ever stops cold. It is the succession of steps moving forward with a purpose that has true meaning in our lives. A baby who is first learning how to walk does not take just one step. His feet will bound forward as if his tiny legs are springs. I remember my children's first steps and seeing their legs trembling from the force of tender new muscles moving for the very first time. A baby's legs are unsure and unsteady, and every so often babies fall, landing softly on their bottoms and bouncing back up again like rubber balls.

Most of our first steps are not baby steps. My first steps here are related to my training in dance, as an adult who was well past the optimal "dance age." Through dance, I came to learn how your own first steps, no matter how large or how small, should always be borne of your own insight and intuition. The inspiration for those steps is always delivered in a small, still, quiet voice that is often impossible not to hear and even more impossible to ignore. Instructions for first steps do not come from a doctor, a counselor, a consultant, a clerk, a clergy member, a coach, a spouse, a friend, a priest or a rabbi. The guidance for first steps always comes from deep within.

Why did I begin to dance as an adult? Every day, I ask myself this question. At first, I was drawn to dance as an accidental discovery. I had been drawn to dance when I was a child, but it was something I never had a chance to do. I have never had a "career" in dance, and it never occurred to me to become a professional dancer. Dance was not on my radar and it did not capture my attention, my imagination or my heart.

Somewhere in the deep recesses of my soul, I had always wanted to dance, but a series of small tragedies stopped me. I do feel that had I wanted to dance badly enough when I was young, I would have made it happen, no matter what my circumstances were at the time. It just wasn't the right time. If I had danced as a young woman, I would not know what I have come to know now.

I think dancing late in life is my destiny. I learn things out on the floor that I cannot seem to learn anywhere else. I learn to be disciplined on days when it does not feel good. I learn to stretch and extend myself when all I want to do is to shrink and contract, the way people do when it is so much easier to settle for less than giving our best.

With creaky bones and bitter smiles, most people become set in their ways, like leafless trees that have lost their branches during their finest hour. I will never be one of them, and neither should you! Pursuing your own physical regimen gives you the discipline to work though all forms of pain in life. Whether the pain is real or imagined, physical or mental, spiritual or existential does not matter. By climbing "steps," we lift ourselves out of despair and reach a higher place of understanding our own humanity.

Let's get to our first steps.

— 1 —

First Steps

My memories of first steps are forever rooted in an old, brown-colored New York tenement where my Irish grandparents lived. It was there, on the sidewalk in front of 67 Jackson Street in Yonkers, where I took my first steps. I can't be sure if this two-story walkup was a classic brownstone. I do recall a tin roof, oversized gutters, bumpy plaster, splintered wall boards, and speckled composite board siding, all the right elements necessary to create a matchstick building that was destined in later years to become a firetrap.

The building did burn down. My grandmother's relocation to a nursing home left the home abandoned and forgotten. No one in my family wanted to own a building in the slums of South Yonkers. The burning of the building was flawlessly timed to a developer's encroachment on the neighborhood, paving the way for a huge "project" to house welfare recipients. There were signs of arson, but no one was on watch and no one was keeping score. There is much more to this story than a simple matter of abandonment and possible arson, but let's just leave it for now and get on to the building's steps.

Inside the tenement, the steps were odd-shaped, uneven; not one seemed to be of the same height. Each step was covered with mottled blue linoleum and had a metal tread that bordered the edge. If you were a child, as I was at the time, the irregularity of each step's height and shape made the steps more precarious to climb. It was easy to miss my footing, which resulted in a misstep, a fall, and a nicked shin. The regular pattern of slight bruises and bumps made me a careful climber of these jagged steps.

I soon learned the more I climbed the steps, the repetition of training made me agile and prone to know where the ruts and sharp edges could propel me into a fall. And if I did fall, I scrambled up quickly without missing a beat or doing something as silly as crying. I've never been very good at crying, which is another story altogether. Let's say I am much more likely to cry out of joy than I am to cry out of pain.

My early memories of dance are more about being high-energy than they are about God, discipline, business, love and art. As a toddler, I danced so enthusiastically, my parents did not want to take me out in public. At restaurants, parties, weddings, or in private homes, I pushed my way out onto whatever floor was there, and danced. I danced with other people or I danced alone. I danced to any type of music or to no music; I even made my own annoying rustling, tapping sound as an accompaniment. I danced for any audience that would watch me, or I danced to the sheer musicality in my own head.

My parents, worn-down and exasperated by my propensity to dance, were embarrassed by my energetic dancing, which made them seem to be out-of-control because they couldn't control me. In family-style restaurants, they pushed me along the seat deep inside the booth, where I would be confined like a prisoner. Still, I always found a way out. I squirmed, slinking down under the table and crawling along the floor, seeing the adults' legs as strong as trees blocking me from getting to the floor, where I could dance. Snakelike, I gyrated and slithered slowly along the floor in between my parents' legs until I finally emerged and easily jumped up from under the table where I launched into my own frenetic version of hip-hop.

As a child, my family and friends called me *Patty*, a *sobriquet* that stuck. A *sobriquet* sounds like it should be a ballet term but it is a nickname, sometimes assumed, that is often given by another. In this case, my sobriquet came about by a well meaning Aunt on the Italian side of the family who was paying back my father for dubbing her *Jo-Jo* as a child. She began calling me *Patty*, and it stuck. A nickname is usually a familiar name, distinct from a pseudonym, which is often assumed as a disguise or cloak protecting one's real identity. I never cared for my sobriquet *Patty*. In the New York lexicon marked by its harsh accent, *Patty* sounded like an Irish treat in honor of St. Patrick's Day, but it is the name all of my childhood friends called me.

A friend in high school, Carmen Canavan, called me *Patty*, but when she called my name it took on a particular lilt as graceful as the way she moved. My early image of dancers was narrowed to this one friend in high school, Carmen Canavan, who wanted to dance. But Carmen's mother did not want her to pursue a career in dance and would not pay for her dance lessons. I knew how important it was for Carmen to dance, so I found a wealthy friend who helped to pay for her lessons. We were barely 17. Carmen and I spent a lot of time roaming Manhattan in pursuit of culture, talking about what life would be like when we were more grown-up, successful and refined.

Aside from Carmen, I did not know any other dancers. To me, dancers were proud, remote, mysterious creatures. To be able to speak with my body or to speak in a physical language seemed to be born of a strange lexicon. I had very little formal training, oh, here and there in fits, jolts and spurts—a sequence of jazz classes or modern dance and aerobics in a gym. During my school years, I took dance more as a way to fill a Physical Education (PE) requirement than as a mind-driven physicality or a pure artistic expression. I knew dance was there, but it was far off in the distance and something I would encounter later on the road up ahead. The desire to dance hid inside of me, like a great buried treasure waiting to be uncovered and explored.

So I came to dance as a latecomer, at an age when the world's most gifted ballerinas have long retired. I started to dance due to a small, simple turn of events, a twist of fate. I took my first steps on a day that started out like every other day, and instead turned into a life-defining experience. Call it an epiphany.

I can pinpoint when I rediscovered ballet. One day in September, I skipped the gym and decided to walk from my home on the top of Queen Anne Hill in Seattle to go as-far-as-I-could. The sky was pure cerulean blue and so cloudless, I could see a horizon of mountains going on forever. Given my many years of cardio training, I knew I could walk a long time.

As I descended onto the flat plane of the Belltown neighborhood, I walked at a fast clip, past many storefronts. One storefront caught my eye because there was movement behind the window. I stepped forward to peer through. I could see inside of a studio where a strange assortment of adults were practicing ballet. Mostly women, a few young men, all shapes and sizes, some wearing torn tights and ripped t-shirts, they stood at the *Barré*; some were my age. It was at that moment when I heard a gentle, but strong, voice tell me I should dance.

Some people think hearing a still, quiet voice is God, and others define the voice as our own intuition. In my family, with its deep history of mental aberrations, hearing voices is no laughing matter and usually means it's time to refill a prescription. But since I was spared the family malady, I took the voice to be something I could ignore. Then it grew louder and more obnoxious. "*Dance!*," it commanded.

"*You get out there and dance!*" I shot back. The voice persisted, "*Dance!*" I protested, "*I'm old, and I have bad knees.*" The voice didn't care: "*Get over it. Dance!*" Don't you love this voice? Aside from being a devoted friend and the one thing you can always count on, the voice can be a ruthless, persistent tormentor that knows the precise buttons to push. It said: *"Get out there and do something different. Dance!"*

Even when we stumble upon a great truth, we tend to rapidly move on, as if we are trying to avoid the scene of an accident, and as if nothing out of the ordinary has happened.

So my initial brush with dance was this *accidental discovery*. Some of your greatest revelations in life will come from accidental discoveries. Many psychics, mystics and religious figures say there are no accidents. If something was meant to be, it's your destiny. I believe there are no accidents, and, more often than not, you did the hard work to put yourself in the right place at the right time for an epiphany to occur.

After my command to dance, I tried to hurry off. I didn't really think about my epiphany at all and treated the experience rather dismissively. Later that week, though, for some inexplicable reason, I felt an impulse to see if I had kept any old dance shoes. I did rummage through the back of my closet to see if I could find any ballet slippers and found a pair in a black & white shoe box, along with my high-heel tap shoes. The last time I tapped, I was pregnant with my son David, who is now twenty-six. I don't even remember why I had ballet slippers in the box. I hadn't worn them in a while. My black leather ballet slippers had hardened with age.

The voice that commanded me to dance is not a stranger or a troubled *ne'er-do-well*. Through the years, I have come to know that this voice, my own intuition, is my best friend, who just happens to be God. And when I haven't listened to this voice, I've gotten into trouble. An equally disturbing prospect is listening to this voice can make my life difficult. Sometimes it wants me to undertake small unpleasant tasks, large unpopular causes or ridiculous onerous projects. The voice can make me feel like Jesus in the Garden of Gethsemane, begging God to let him pass the cup. He really does not want to be the Son of God and he does not want to endure crucifixion. The voice will make you live out your own destiny, whether you like it or not, and will nag you until it gets its way. Now it was telling me to get out there and dance. Sometimes I really hate this voice.

The next week, on Saturday, I returned to the studio, which was named *Belltown Ballet*. When I walked in, I was literally taking steps so small that no one could guess just how large and grand a movement would soon unfold.

I was wearing my black spandex bike tights, the same pair that I always wore to the gym, and a camisole top. My feet felt strange, encased in the black leather ballet slippers that had hardened to be as stiff as turtle shells.

Belltown Ballet, not a large dance studio, was jam-packed with all types and sizes of bodies. Some dancers wore sleek leotards, black tights and sheer ballet skirts, others wore ripped and run tights revealing bare flesh, and others wore baggy sweatpants and oversized T-shirts. The male students in the class wore tight, form-fitting unitards that showed their well-developed derriere, and full frontal endowment. One young man wore climbing tights and socks with Birkenstocks and looked like he was ready to take off on a hike. I was relieved to see him remove his sandals. I knew enough about ballet to know that one should not wear shoes, flats, heels or sandals. I knew we should wear soft ballet slippers. At least I had that going for me.

A wooden *Barré* ran the length of a wall that had windows looking into a narrow passageway flanked on one side by plywood rafters. Yellowed garage-sale-style paintings depicting kitschy renditions of classical ballet hung lopsided on the wall. The floor was painted gunmetal gray and seemed to grow harder under my feet each moment that I stood there. Thick tape on the floor had been painted over and in some sections was coming up.

I did not want to look at myself in the mirror. I studiously avoided my reflection and instead focused on the teacher, who appeared to be about my age. Annie de Vuono was extraordinarily slender, wore no makeup, had long, flowing gray hair and the unlined, rosy skin of a child. She lifted her leg into the air in a full extension reaching 180 degrees in a straight line to the ceiling. Some of the dancers at the *Barré* gasped and giggled at the fact that anyone could possibly have an extension that high.

At the *Barré*, we were doing one of the most fundamental ballet steps of all—the *tendu*. Both the standing leg and the moving leg must be kept straight. Easier said than done! The tendu requires a well-honed pointed toe to lead the foot in a glide, along a straight line to the side along the floor, moving in and out repeatedly, then returning to the starting position. Even the simple movement of sliding one leg straight along the floor can be excruciating for a beginner. Just imagine keeping your feet perfectly pointed, both legs straight, your posture totally erect, pulling in your abdomen and seat. Your working arm is perfectly suspended in the air, with the other arm holding on to the *Barré* gently. My "other" arm that clutched the *Barré* was locked in a death grip and looked very much like I was holding onto a life preserver as I slowly sank into the ocean. I was drowning, and I knew it.

I felt my teacher Annie's eyes appraise me at the *Barré*. I was unable to point my toe for as long as it took to slide it out straight and then back into first position. As I think about it now, I really did not know where first position was located. My foot would not point, my legs would not stay straight and I wobbled, failing miserably to return to first position in the same amount of time as all the other feet moving fast on the floor.

Just at this moment Annie began shouting, "Knees! Knees! Knees! Don't bend your knees. Both knees must be kept straight! Your standing leg is working as hard as your moving leg!"

I tried to keep my standing leg prone, and the more I forced it to be straight, the more it seemed to collapse under me. Soon it did not feel like a leg at all and it took on the feel of a disembodied stump, like the remnants of a dead tree.

Then she was yelling "Toes! Point those toes!" She crouched low to the ground like a sleek cat. She was so close to me, I could feel her breath. She pointed to my floppy foot and told me to return it crisply to first position, as if I was closing a door.

Annie observed me closely and asked me if I had taken ballet. I nodded and said, "Back in college," but the reality was that my college training had been so brief and so long ago, it might as well never have happened. She studied me for a moment, and looked down toward the floor where she spied my feet, stuck in lizard-hard black leather ballet slippers and she said, "You have great feet. Don't fuck with me." At that instant, I knew I wanted her to be my teacher.

From the outside, when you see dancers doing steps, you sometimes fool yourself into thinking, *I can do that. Just let me try.* But without any training, you quickly find that your body just will not move. It will not do even one little thing that you ask. Your feet will not point. Your working leg will not stay straight. Your standing leg will not feel stable. Your hips will be thrust to the side. All of the little muscles that help you to balance are dormant. You are off-center. You cannot do a damn thing.

A lesson in grace—training, or call it practice and polish, is a critical part of everything we do. How often we can fool ourselves into thinking that we can skate by without trying too hard. You may get away with it once or twice, but never for the long run, which is what it takes to build a business or to build a life. There is no substitute for hard work and discipline—the day-in, day-out work.

Taking first steps means doing the steps every day. The first step can easily be a misstep and will yield very little. What is much more difficult is the process of starting up, a new beginning, a new day, a new year and doing the hard work of doing the steps constantly and continuously, for an indefinite period over time. The step of the cat *(pas de chat*) or* the step of the horse *(pas de cheval*)* are not only part of my unconscious lexicon but are deeply rooted in my muscle memory. I practice these dance steps several times a week. And some days, for no explicable reason, I do these steps better than I do them on other days.*

It is never too late to learn how to dance! I have come to know that training in dance is so challenging and so rewarding, it makes all other steps in life—no matter how difficult—easier to master and to endure. When we are learning to dance, using long-dormant muscles, our legs will quiver, like babies who are learning to walk for the first time.

Speaking of babies, Sarah is my youngest child. I do not remember the exact day we started dancing together. I wish I had captured the moment and committed it to memory, but at the time I did not know that we were taking first steps together. I do remember the two of us bounding into the car on many cold rainy nights, flapping our coats and shaking mud from our shoes so we could get to dance class in time to get a place—for two—at the *Barré*. Sometimes you can take steps and not know they are first steps.

Sarah and I started taking dance classes together at the funky *Belltown Ballet* studio in Seattle. Since then we have danced in many studios. Eventually, we found ourselves taking classes at Pacific Northwest Ballet (PNB), at eXitSPACE dance studio, and at *Steps on Broadway* in New York City. Sarah is as passionate about dance as she is passionate about astronomy. She says that passion means that you love something so much, it moves you to tears and even if you don't feel like doing anything, you

---

* http://www.abt.org/education/dictionary/index.html

move forward somehow. When you really love something, it defines who you are, and you cannot stop taking small steps because you find out something new about yourself that you never knew before.

My love of dance deepened my relationship with my daughter. I remember our positioning, standing together at the *Barré*, cleaved into two bodies instead of one, forming pretzel-shapes like musical notes. I remember that she was a beautiful young girl with long, brown hair and a smile that radiated from the fullness of her heart. I admired her from afar to the extent that sometimes I forgot she was my daughter. Before long, we trained together to be in the same dance performance, even though it took me five attempts to get a step that she could learn in one.

Taking first steps is never easy. You can be stupid about it, or scared, or even thick-headed, but you must do it all the same. Taking first steps requires the courage to stand firmly on your feet to find your position. Taking first steps is always a time to test your mettle. Whether you are being interviewed for a job or by the press, or starting a new job with a client, or walking into a networking group for the first time, you may feel more than just a little awkward. You may experience profound moments of fear. If you do not occasionally experience these emotions, either you are lying or you are not very good at what you do. If you truly care about doing something well, then you must worry in a good way that will fuel you to do your best work.

Last year, a woman walked into the ballet class I was in. She looked to be in her mid-fifties. She wore a long, flowing black transparent ballet skirt and her shoes were new. She seemed very nervous and kept fidgeting at the *Barré*. She froze and would not go across the floor. Then she left. I wanted to go after her. I wanted to call out, "You will never be any good if you do not give yourself permission to be bad. You are not making a fool of yourself at all." When you are of a certain age, you should no longer be stopped by the kinds of feelings you had when you were in middle school. We all feel the same way you do. We are all here to make mistakes. We are learning to become dancers. We are learning to be better people. We are learning to live. If we don't learn to live now, the moment will move on and leave us behind.

Learning to dance means learning how to take steps. When we are first beginning to dance and learning a new step, we tend to go slowly and take one step at a time. But once we start moving, there is a succession of steps that become fluid and create a complete phrase of movement, carving out the new direction of where we are going, even if we are only traveling across the floor. Once we learn the movement, and no longer get stuck on a step, we are free.

When I first started to dance, I didn't have a guidebook or a road map to let me know what I should expect. I found the classic book, *How to Dance Forever: Surviving Against the Odds*, (NY: HarperCollins, 1988). Written by the famed dancer and choreographer Daniel Nagrin, this is a wonderful book for dancers who have trained their entire lives and want to learn technique to prolong their lives-in-dance. I read the book from cover to cover until the pages were worn, marked-up and dog-eared. But it does not offer guidance and wisdom to older dancers like you and me who are just beginning to dance.

The dance world itself is youth-oriented and does not encourage older non-dancers who are beginning to learn how to dance. There are commonly held myths that only the young should dance. I found this comment on a blog and it amused me. The writer, who is only 23, wrote, *"Basically I'm wanting to start dancing again and just wondering how all you 'older' dancers do it. I feel a bit old (just turned 23) but really miss it. I don't mind being in a class with 'little ones,' but just worried I'll look a bit odd! Any comments would be great."*

This young woman did not get any comments. I wonder what she would say if she knew how many classes I have walked into between Seattle and New York City and found people in their retirement years who take a dance class every day.

In every studio I have been to, whether it is a professional ballet school like Pacific Northwest Ballet (PNB) or a small studio on the west side of Manhattan, there are dance communities made up of amateur dancers, hobbyists, and people who, for one reason or another, just want to dance. You get to know other people by routinely showing up at the same dance classes. And all of a sudden, one day, you are part of a community.

We are fat, fit, thin; some of us used to be professional dancers and some of us have not danced in years. A few are here every day like clockwork, no matter what. We come from all walks of life, professions, economic backgrounds; we are building businesses, living, working, trying to find a job, caretaking for the sick and the dying, tending to the injured. Some of us are sick and dying ourselves. We are raising children, loving our friends and family. We come in all shapes and sizes; we are of all ages and abilities. We are here because we share one thing in common: we want to dance.

When I go to New York, I take classes at *Steps on Broadway* with Robert Atwood. Every time I take his class, I see Miriam, a teacher who recently retired from Hunter College. She is battling arthritis and takes a ballet class every day to loosen her joints and to give her life structure. Whenever I see Miriam, she always gives me a big smile and says, "Hi, you're back." And I feel like I have come home.

My not-so-secret life in dance has enabled me to meet the most interesting people: former judges and prosecutors, a neurosurgeon who works in the trauma unit of Harborview Medical Center. At least two of my dance friends are thriving despite having degenerative disorders of the central nervous systems;

several are battling or recovering from cancer. They are all not only taking first steps, they are stepping on, using their love of dance to enhance their businesses, their occupations, and their lives. All of us are engaged in a dance of life. All of us are dancing for life, dancing to live, to grieve, to survive, to feel passion, and to experience profound joy. In our hearts, dancing means feeling a wild rush of exhilaration where we embrace the feeling of freedom.

Some people have sickness, disabilities; physical and mental limitations that you might think would hinder them from dancing. There is the story of Barbara Willis, who has taught dance for most of her life. Her own diagnosis of Parkinson's disease soon taught her that the more she continued to dance, the more her symptoms were lessened. Now in her 70s and living in Colorado, Barbara Willis teaches other students who have Parkinson's disease to dance. "It's amazing how, if you have a tremor, it will disappear during this song," Willis tells her students. "These moves are difficult for us, but the music overcomes it." Each week, Willis and her students practice balance and movement. They dance in rhythm with the music, to combat a disease that threatens to rob them of their power to move.*

So what is holding you back from dancing? It is never too late to learn to dance! The same truth holds for all other aspects of life. It is never too late to fall in love, to start a business, to grow your business, or to make a new friend. It is never too late to change your life, your job, where you live, or your calling. It is never too late to forgive yourself or someone else. Dance is a lot like love; the more you do it, the more you want to do. Dance can be the highest form of art and expression that you can achieve.

---

* Controlled Moves Sun Journal June 28 2009 http://www.newbernsj.com/articles/disease-46186-parkinson-willis.html

Dance makes me better in all things. Dance makes me endure all things. Dance makes me a believer in taking what is ordinary about myself and turning it into something extraordinary. *I dance just because I can.* It is important to tell you: *If I can dance, so can you.*

When I first started dancing, I did not know that dance would help me to solve the most complicated business problems and develop a vision for the future. I did not know that I would learn how the fundamental principles of ballet could be applied to business in a way that helped me to explore excellence. I did not know that dance would help me connect with a God who has a special place in his heart for people—the dancers of this world—who move the earth.

— 2 —

Positioning

In Yonkers, my grandmother's tenement had a front stoop, a back stoop, and heavy wooden doors covered with layers of brittle oil paint that were thick enough to ward off street crime and still keep all of the family's secrets locked inside. And we had many secrets, none of which seemed to be all that earth-shattering to a four-year-old girl. We downplayed what was bad, wrong or awful in our lives and pumped up what was good, right and excellent in order to reach far beyond the quagmire of the neighborhood. A certain upbeat, polished stoicism prevailed. It's no wonder I eventually went into public relations. The tenement's steps taught me the art of storytelling and how to spin well while always downplaying my emotions and keeping a straight face.

My high school years were reckless and crazy. In my junior year, I entered Blessed Sacrament Academy, a small all-girl Catholic school where the nuns were cloistered. I won't mention where I had been going to school before then. I was a troubled teenager, a rebel with many causes. Rather than delving into the details, let's just leave that and get on with the **Steps**.

Even though the high school cliques were already formed, most of the girls were welcoming to a newcomer. They gave me a new sobriquet, "Pat Vac," a name I despised because I felt it did not define who I was. I circled away from the complicated emotional intricacies of the cliques and found a friend who was quiet, shy, sophisticated, and a loner. Carmen Canavan wanted to be a dancer. Carmen had lived in Barcelona, Spain, where her father had been assigned for a year. She had a beautiful, polished way of speaking, and none of the squawking New York accent that dominated the speech of most girls from Yonkers and the Bronx.

Carmen wanted to dance, and I wanted to write. Carmen had already trained extensively in ballet, and I had already written reams of poetry, a play, and a novel called "Beneath the Passion of the Angelic Mystery Rose," in which the main character, Andrea Verrone, encountered one obstacle after another while she explored the truth and meaning of life. It was based on my own true story, and my early stab at writing *spin*. Even then I knew that the best *spin* is crafted from the truth.

I don't know why I did not want to dance. I think I thought I had my chance to dance and the opportunity had passed. As strange as it seems, my opportunity to dance had not passed at all. A whole lifetime or two later, the first time I walked into a ballet studio as an adult was on a clear September day the week after my epiphany telling me to dance. When I first began to learn about positioning and placement, my feet felt strange on the floor. My feet had always been sensitive and ticklish, and so, through the years, I always preferred to wear a thick cushion like a *Nike* air sole as a protective buffer. I was not keen to have my feet hugging any floor, even in a ballet studio.

Five years later, after 1,500 hours of ballet training, I have learned to love the feel of the floor under my feet. More than anything, I have grown to love the experience of using my feet to push away from the floor and jump into the air. The legendary choreographer Martha Graham said, "Think of the magic of that foot, comparatively small, upon which your whole weight rests. It's a miracle, and the dance is a celebration of that miracle."

Regarding positioning, you probably thought I would talk about the five basic positions in ballet. If you want to learn about the five basic positions of ballet, take a class or watch a video. If you want to get esoteric, look at some of the works created by another legendary modern dance choreographer, Merce Cunningham, who is credited for identifying the five positions of the back: upright, curved, arched, twisted and tilted.

But only showing the basic positions in dance for your arms or feet or back will tell you nothing about yourself. There is much more to be said about the thought and training that goes into positioning. Positioning is much more than how you stand, or how you place your arms and feet.

Positioning is how you want the world to see you, whether in life or in business, whether you have an audience or not. Positioning is how you will be seen from the outside, and that reflects who you are deep down inside, as a person. Martha Graham describes the concept of theater: "Theater is a verb before it is a noun, an act before it is a place." How well you position yourself before the world has everything to do with how you see yourself. You must know your own story before you can tell it to the world.

Another great ballet concept related to positioning has to do with turnout. A physical "turnout" is the rotation of the leg, which starts at the hips and causes the knee and foot to turn outward, away from the center of the body.

In business or in life, the expression "turnout" refers to the outcome. The number of people who *turn out* for an election or an event, or to buy a product, is an indicator of success. In ballet, it is quite the opposite. Turnout is the beginning, the placement that is essential to all other steps. The first step must be the logical outgrowth of well-placed feet and hips. The turnout is evident in how you stand in first position. Your legs are pressed very close together and your feet can point in a V-shape or take on a perfect 180-degree line. My first ballet teacher Annie de Vuono says, "From the moment you put your foot on the brake to park your car and enter the ballet studio, until the moment the class ends, you are in permanent turnout."

Dancers spend a lot of time working on their turnout. Great turnout enhances many ballet moves, from the ability to jump high to the ability to do multiple turns. Whether you dance or not, you too need to spend a lot of time working on your metaphorical turnout. By choosing the correct positioning, you will get a good *turnout* for your personal life and for your business.

Positioning is how you want your audience to see you: from a stage, from a board room, at a networking meeting; how well you have positioned yourself means you are giving people the ability to clearly see who you are, and who you are not.

Positioning means where you are physically located. You are on a stage, in a board room or at a networking meeting because you have chosen to be there, to keep company with the people who will be there. You have made this physical place your own brand *milieu*.

In ballet, positioning is the ultimate branding statement. In the business world, how well you position yourself is what will establish your brand. It is your initial starting point. It takes hard work, lots of training and discipline to achieve and establish the correct positioning.

Another deeper aspect of positioning is revealed by asking yourself how you want your audience to see you. Positioning means you must be certain about your own identity. How can you be alive and have confusion about your background, your abilities, your talents, your skills, what you are passionate about, and what you want to do with your life? How can you expect *me* to know who you are if *you* don't know who you are? How can I make time for a phantom?

Martha Graham said, "First we have to believe, and then

we believe." Father Peter Moore, an Episcopalian priest I knew, said, "If you act as though you have faith, then eventually faith will be given to you." The message coming from the dancer and the priest is similar: you must act as though you believe in yourself before anyone else can believe in you.

Positioning is not only who you are and how you define yourself. Positioning is ultimately about how you will play to your audience. It does not matter whether you are a dancer, a medical doctor, a judge, a journalist, a scientist, an economist, a management consultant, or an entertainer; you must always know who your audience is, and consider their complex set of emotional needs.

Before I began to dance, I was always physically disciplined. I worked hard to stay fit, and never was one to sit in front of the television with a big bowl of potato chips. I was in the gym five days a week for at least hour and a half workouts, such as routine cardio and lifting weights. I took long walks, and found ways to stretch the outer edges of my complete physicality. I like to move and to express myself physically. Movement makes me feel alive.

Over twenty years ago, I was doing heavy weight training combined with a steady regimen of high-impact aerobics classes. My knees were causing me pain and swelling up like balloons. A sports medicine doctor told me if I didn't stop what I was doing, I would need knee replacements by the time I was forty. He advised me to stop any physical activity, short of walking, that involved my knees, and asked if I had a house with steps. Yes, my old house had 17 steps inside. "Climbing steps is out of the question," the doctor said. "Sell your house."

Even though he advised me to sell my house, I didn't listen. I am still living in the same craftsman-style home with its 17 steps. Now that I think of it, every home I have ever lived in has had an enormous number of steps. As you will soon see, I have a deep spiritual affinity for climbing steps. Climbing steps is as essential to my life as the earth I stand on and the air I breathe. Steps are deeply ingrained in the essence of who I am.

The sports medicine doctor had totally misjudged his target audience. This is bad positioning. There is a simple lesson in grace about giving advice: always consider your audience. This expert was giving sound advice, based on his own limited knowledge; it was just all wrong for me. Despite his poor advice, he allowed me to learn a powerful lesson in grace: before you open your mouth to give advice, always consider your intended recipient, your target audience. This doctor failed to consider his audience and only talked about what he knew. He didn't study me—the person who would receive his measured words of wisdom. He didn't seem to "get" that I thought of myself as an athlete of sorts and did not want to be told to come to a complete stop. If he had asked a few questions, he would have understood: I would never stop.

During my first adult ballet class, Annie de Vuono struck a profound position that revealed her style as a teacher. What is exceptional about Annie is her ability to make you feel that by dancing, you are creating beauty and magic in the world. She makes you feel beautiful and inspires her students to evolve into beautiful dancers. Since my first class with Annie, I have taken over 500 ballet classes and I have had about 30 ballet instructors, some gifted, some not. I have taken hundreds of classes with some teachers, and only one class with other teachers, due to timing or circumstances. In every class, no matter how great or how poor the instruction, I have learned at least one important lesson about life, business and, of course, dance.

Some lessons were beautiful and profound, others I wished I did not have to learn, still others I was bound to repeat because I kept making the same mistakes. It is important to emphasize that *no lesson was every wasted*. Every class offered a lesson in positioning, in how to stand correctly. Even if no one is watching, you come to set your own standard and begin to know when you are standing correctly.

Ballet training is the foundation of all dance training because it teaches your body which muscles need to be developed and strengthened in order to perform any form of movement. Every dance movement, no matter what style, requires flexibility, fluidity and physics. If the proper physics is not cast into action, then you cannot achieve your positioning.

What you achieve in dance, in life and in business springs from your positioning. If dance is a metaphor for life and business, then I can ask: Where are you standing? How are you standing? How are you holding your arms? How far are you standing from the *Barré*? How close are you standing to your audience? What do you plan to communicate to your audience? In dance, in life and in business, you must think in a way that reaches for the highest level in yourself. In spite of any handicaps, mental challenges or physical limitations, you must realize that your mindset will determine your ability to explore excellence.

In every ballet class I have ever taken, from the first one during that fateful day in September, to the one I took last Saturday, I have experienced both failure and success. Dance has taught me that it is okay to make mistakes, so long as my intent is to always strive for excellence. Dance has given me permission to make mistakes in training so I can achieve greater clarity in how to position myself in life and in business.

To truly embrace the concept of positioning, you have to ask yourself: can you afford to make mistakes? You came out of school with certifications and credentials; you are supposed to know your profession inside out. Your profession is stable, an immutable force, but then ten years later there is no longer much need for your skills. You have the right to reassess who you are. You have the right to reinvent yourself. You have the right to experiment with your life and your business. You will make mistakes. And making mistakes can be the right thing to do. Just don't make a habit of it, because sooner or later, you have to hit your marks. Whenever people are paying you for your work, though, the mistakes must drop off and your error rate must immediately go down to zero. You can't strike correct positioning unless you hit your marks.

Many people who are good at what they do are afraid to take risks for fear of not doing a good job. Learning how to be bad at something can actually be a good thing. I know a surgeon who took jazz classes because it gave her the freedom to make mistakes with her dance that she could never afford to make in the operating room. Here is my advice to you: make a mistake. No, don't make a mistake. It's a paradox, in the same way that ballet training can help you to be a better business person. Pursue excellence. Pursue the ideal. You will rarely hit the ideal, but if you do your best work, you will get *beautifully* close.

When I first started training in ballet, it was hard to embrace positioning. One teacher, Bruce Wells at Pacific Northwest Ballet (PNB), has an incredible way of teaching me to find my place on the floor. In class, he always says, "Eyes up." After a time, my eyes focus upward and take the rest of my body along, and soon I am reaching higher, extending tall and focusing upward. He did not have to tell the dancers that if we kept our eyes up, surely our bodies would follow. It reminds me of what Martha Graham once said: "I did not want to be a tree, a flower or a wave. In a dancer's body, we as audience must see ourselves, not the imitated behavior of everyday actions, not the phenomenon of nature, not exotic creatures from another planet, but something of the miracle that is a human being."

Dancers will often tell you that dance is a language and the ultimate artistic form of communication. Martha Graham said, "The body says what words cannot." She describes dance communication as "the hidden language of the soul of the body." I have come to view dance as a way to define my position with razor-sharp precision. Ballet training has given me a certain practiced talent in learning how to put a fence around my emotions, a temporary place to house my feelings and to define the outer perimeters of my position. I may acknowledge that I am feeling awkward, but now—when I am in the moment and about to dance—is simply not the time to deal with my emotions.

Temporary suppression gives me the freedom to review everything later, as if I am looking at a video after the performance is over. When you are in training, in dance, in business, in life, sometimes it is best to review your performance in retrospect. Look at your performance as if it is a video. Study your plays and your moves with detachment so that the next time, you can improve your positioning.

Once I interviewed Kent Stowell, who, with Francia Russell, was the co-founder of the Pacific Northwest Ballet (PNB). He talked about the anxiety inherent in doing one's best work. "With choreography, there is always a huge risk, but it is a risk well-taken. When I am creating a new piece, I always feel like I am on the right road if I feel nervous. A certain kind of 'working' anxiety tells me that the process is working." Stowell was speaking about a new work he had choreographed for the dance company *Seattle Dance Project*, but his thoughts can apply to every aspect of doing your best work in life or business.

Kent Stowell also noted, "With choreography, you begin to see metaphors with the creation of other things in life." The constant training inherent in positioning enables you to do your best work, no matter what emotions you are feeling. In a ballet class, the work at the *Barré* always includes a *Rond de Jambe** sequence. Both legs are perfectly straight; all movement must originate from your hip. The toe of your working foot does not rise off the ground and stays pointed while passing in an arc beyond the fourth position to the front and cycling through to the fourth position to the back. You could walk into a class anywhere in the world, and sooner or later, the *Barré* sequence of exercises will include a *Rond de Jambe*. By doing this exercise repeatedly, over time, you strengthen your standing leg and increase the turnout in both legs. By doing one more *Rond de Jambe* sequence, over time, you are training yourself to use your tension and anxiety as fuel for your passion: your life or your business.*

In every ballet class I have taken, I have experienced some fear, trepidation and a sense of awe when I enter the room. There is a certain anxiety about having to perform, wondering, "Will I perform well? Will I perform at all?" As I later found out, this performance anxiety is not restricted to dance neophytes, but is universal among even the most gifted and experienced dancers. There is always this little seed of doubt when your intent is to do good work, and if you are intent on raising the *Barré,* so to speak, then your intent must be to do your best work.

I have walked into studios where my teachers were living dance legends and the room was full of professional dancers. I have walked into a studio where I am the only person who started ballet training later in life; I am the least technically competent dancer in the room. The professional ballet world, like the movie world in Hollywood, worships youth and discards the old. *But this was not the ballet world I had entered, I told myself, it was simply a ballet class.* When I'm in the moment, I can only focus on being completely present and knowing where my positioning is on the floor. I need to know where the other dancers are located around me. I need to know my space, as

---

* http://www.abt.org/education/dictionary/index.html

it shifts in time and in form while we are all moving together across the floor. By positioning myself in this brand milieu, I have no choice but to do my best work. And by doing my best work, I am establishing who I am as a person, and ultimately, how I will be perceived by the world.

After hundreds of hours of training, something deep within me changed. When I moved across the floor, I began to feel great joy. I began to feel as if I was reaching for a reality much higher than myself. I realized that dance had changed me, and had given me a focus point so intense that it took me out of myself, and yet, at the same time, required all of me. Aside from my physical training at the *Barré*, I have been training my mind to handle all of life's situations in a more graceful and compassionate way. My ability to learn new steps has allowed me to experience lessons in grace. I am more compassionate because I know that sometimes, no matter how hard I try to do something, I may not get the step. But then on the next attempt, the step comes to me so fluidly, it is as if I have been doing it my entire life. And this reality about dance is so unexpected and such a delightful surprise, I have come to believe that to achieve your best positioning in life, you should dance!

— 3 —
Small Adjustments

I always return to my first steps, which are forever rooted in an old New York tenement that no longer exists anywhere other than in my mind. I can recall the scent of the neighborhood, a combination of car exhaust, hot asphalt, creosote, and the humid swell of greenery from the few remaining elm trees lingering behind on Jackson Street. I can see my grandmother's building so vividly, with its tin roof, oversized gutters, bumpy plaster, splintered wall boards, and speckled composite board siding. I see the front stoop made entirely of concrete and the chain link fence that kept my grandmother safe during the years when the neighborhood transitioned from being ethnic, hardworking *working class* and prosperous to poor, drug-addicted and *ghetto*. The swinging of the pendulum from *working class* to *ghetto* transformed the concrete guts of the neighborhood from clean and quaint to garbage-infested and covered with graffiti.

Through the years, I have come to know if you grow up climbing steps in an old New York tenement, you learn to demand much more from yourself and others. The hard part is struggling with this demand and still learning how to be elegant, graceful and compassionate with all the people who will be dismissive of your steps, or worse, take your steps for granted or resent you for having the desire to climb steps in the first place. I have come to know that my desire to climb steps is a powerful metaphor for my desire to explore excellence.

Do you welcome criticism? Most people do not. And it does not matter whether the criticism is well-meaning and constructive. You would not be human if you did not feel a little sting from being criticized. Corrections in ballet, though, are actually compliments! It means that your teacher cares enough about you to take the time to help you to become a better dancer. It means that you have promise. *The more corrections you receive in ballet, the better.*

The small incremental improvements that you make in ballet are the same small adjustments you should be making in business. It is all about improvement. Small, subtle, seemingly insignificant changes made over time eventually culminate to become enormous improvements over time.

In our culture, particularly in business, there is the tendency to *overcorrect*: in the financial and housing markets, in politics and government, and in our social trends. If the regulations are too relaxed and there is some sort of catastrophe, we swing all the way to the opposite direction and become hyper-strict and inflexible.

Case studies abound. One not-very-bright terrorist tries to blow up a plane by striking a match on his shoe. As a result, everyone in the entire world must take off their shoes before boarding an airplane. BP Oil causes a disastrous oil gusher in the Gulf of Mexico and the government responds by cancelling all future drilling plans, which helps escalate the cost of fuel at the gas pump. Our government leaders swing back and forth like a pendulum, anointing the Democrats to do what the Republicans could not do, throwing them out and reeling the Republicans back in, and then the whole cycle keeps repeating. Each party attempts to derail the other without approaching consensus so we can all work together to solve the serious issues that threaten our national security: the national debt ceiling, our deteriorating natural resources, the destruction of our environment, the wars in Afghanistan and Iraq.

Our housing market crashes after years of giving mortgages to people who never had the resources to make the monthly payments. During the height of the housing boom, people without jobs or savings could easily get a mortgage. After the crash, people with great jobs, plenty of savings and good credit are routinely denied mortgages. The chief hallmark of our culture is its ability to deliver a *backlash effect*. The pendulum swings wildly to the left, then wildly to the right on almost every issue, without ever achieving balance.

During the course of ballet training, a dancer learns to make one small adjustment at a time. Ballet training is the opposite of a *backlash effect* of wildly swinging from one extreme to the other. In ballet, as in business, a succession of incremental, barely perceptible changes sustained over time will produce the long-lasting, desired results that, over the course of time, become a major paradigm shift.

It was my fate to learn dancing by studying for five years with many teachers in both Seattle and New York. It is like meeting everyone you would ever need to know in business. It is akin to mastering all the essential reading in your area of expertise. You gain a different nugget of wisdom from each person and every source. For example, at a ballet class at Steps on Broadway in New York, I learned from my teacher Kathleen Smith that I was not turning-out in extension while stretching my legs on the *Barré*.

One can never underestimate the power of a small adjustment. For the first three years of training, my body struggled to embrace an *Assemblé*.[*] Every teacher I have had said: "Just

---

[*] http://www.abt.org/education/dictionary/index.html

assemble your legs in the air and land in fifth position." Assemblé—*As the foot goes into the air the dancer pushes off the floor with the supporting leg, extending the toes. Both legs come to the ground simultaneously in the fifth position.* "Assemble in the air," teachers would demonstrate, their arms slicing across one another like scissors.

One Thursday morning in New York, I took a class with Robert Atwood at Steps on Broadway. Mr. Atwood is an excellent communicator and does not spout French terms. Rather, he defines each movement as a shape: *smaller, longer, rounder, taller*. He did not describe the Assemblé as assembling in the air. Instead, he described the first part of the *Assembl*é when your working leg darts out in full extension, your pointed foot brushes the floor and into the air, and so does your supporting leg, *at the same time.* For me, this small adjustment made all the difference in my ability to learn the coordination of the movement. Mr. Atwood had described a starting point precisely, instead of just saying, "Assemble in the air."*

One of my favorite corrections was in a class taught by Julie Tobiason, who had been a prima ballerina at Pacific Northwest Ballet (PNB). She described the movement of your upper body as if you are floating on top of water, treading through water, pushing water away, becoming one with water. The water metaphor captured strength and stability, and yet was fluid and could shape-shift into many forms, from solid and hard to gentle and delicate. Dance is like water.

After you spend time training, you almost hunger for the teacher's corrections. They are the teacher's acknowledgment that you are doing the hard work necessary to become a better dancer. You must fully understand all of the nuances of the communication, though, which is more complex than it

---

* http://www.abt.org/education/dictionary/

seems. Once, in a class at Pacific Northwest Ballet (PNB), Meg Potter corrected me. She showed the line of how I held my arms overhead in high fifth position, which is the classic pose held by porcelain ballerinas on little music boxes. But from across the room, without glasses, I could not clearly see myself in the mirror, so I could not embrace the full benefit of her correction. You can get the greatest advice in the world, but if you cannot see what is wrong, the proverbial seed falls to barren ground.

Six months later, I happened to be in New York over the weekend. I took a Sunday morning ballet class with Pamela Probisco. After she explained the alignment of the arms as emanating from the *latissimus dorsi muscles* in the middle and side of my back, I was able to understand the alignment of my arms. Before then I had been focusing on my arms themselves instead of embracing the origin of the movement.

It took six months before I embraced the full benefit of Meg Potter's correction to the way I held my arms over my head. Sometimes you are immediately able to make a correction, or it might take many more classes and training until you are ready to make the adjustment.

A directive to make a small adjustment might not always be clear in the instruction of exactly what needs to be done. If you don't completely understand a correction, it may be necessary to consult with your teacher after class. If you are not ready to embody the entire correction, a good teacher can show you a starting point, in the same way Mr. Atwood was able to describe an *Assemblé* in greater detail by breaking it down, rather than by simply saying, "Assemble your feet in the air," or Ms. Probisco was able to describe the origin of an arm movement in my back.

In business, you may be aware of an adjustment that needs to be made. You might have an employee who is not working up to potential or to the standards you have set for the company, and yet you cannot immediately replace this person, even though you know immediately doing so will make your business better. Sometimes you are not intellectually ready or able to see the adjustment that needs to be made. You might have a "wait and see" attitude. Will the emerging pattern tell you that an adjustment must be made? A small adjustment can only be made when the timing is right for you to make the change.

If only our leaders in business and in government spent some time at a ballet *Barré*, they might have a sense of understanding the power and discipline inherent in making small adjustments. Twyla Tharp once said, "I don't think politicians should be allowed into power who are not familiar with their bodies, because that's where our bottom line is. And I know that they would make totally different decisions if they felt responsible simply for their own bodies."

If the *backlash effect* is the chief hallmark of our culture, then it is important to ponder that the true essence of ballet training is rooted in the desire to make small adjustments. If more people were trained as dancers, they would understand the concept of making small incremental adjustments instead of making radical overcorrections that result in a weaker positioning. The positioning created from a *backlash* is never balanced or functionally sound.

In ballet, you are taking one step at a time. You are also taking multiple steps. And if you are good, it appears as though you are leaping over many steps, but you are in fact, not skipping any steps at all. You have heard the expression "leapfrogging" in business; that's where you make such a spectacular strategic move, it appears as though you have leapt over all of the basic steps. *Leapfrog* moves are illusory. *Leapfrogging* means you are so well-trained that you are able to make doing something very hard look easy. There is an old adage in business that the woman who goes to bed one night and finds herself suddenly famous in the morning has not been asleep for ten years. To make *leapfrogging* appear to be effortless means you must make many small adjustments over a long span of time.

One summer day, after I had taken classes for five years, Annie de Vuono's sister Mary Englund watched our class. Afterward, she commented to me that my extension was high and looked effortless, and that I must be a natural dancer. I thought her comment was very revealing about the process of ballet; it had taken me five years of hard work and a multitude of small adjustments to achieve any sort of extension!

It takes time before the body is able to internalize and fully actualize a small adjustment. Sometimes it is one step forward, two steps backward.

Making small adjustments is the essence of growth. But a great correction can change your life.

For example, I wanted to be able to do a pirouette *en dehors* from fourth position for the longest time.* I had not seen Annie de Vuono since I first took her intermediate class two years earlier at Belltown Ballet. As soon as I found her again (she was now teaching at eXitSPACE), she corrected me. I had been repeatedly trying to turn from the wrong leg. The difficulty in learning to rewire a bad pattern requires hours of practice and devotion. For two years, I had been using the wrong leg to turn the wrong way!

My first turns did not emerge until I had trained enough to pull my working leg up *en passé*, with the tip of the toe placed lightly to the inside thigh of my standing leg. After three years of training, I could only do inside turns *en dedans* with any degree of regular reliability. Then after four years, I could do a pirouette or outside turn *en dehors* with greater reliability. This

---

* The pirouette is a *whirl or spin. A complete turn of the body on one foot, on point or demi-pointe. Pirouettes are performed en dedans, turning inward toward the supporting leg, or en dehors, turning outward in the direction of the raised leg.* http://www.abt.org/education/dictionary/

notion of *greater reliability* means that more often than not, I could do a turn with some technical precision.

The pirouette is a physical marvel; its perfection still eludes me. I recall one of my classes at PNB when Bruce Wells told a company dancer—who had whipped out six pirouettes—that he was working too hard to dominate his turns. "The pirouette is like a diva," he said, "You cannot make her do anything that she does not want to do. You must submit to her will."

You may not have the opportunity to wrestle with the majestic pirouette to see if you and your business and your brand are in alignment. You may not have ballet training to use as a ballast, an example of the constant need to make small adjustments in business. You might have to hire a business coach or a consultant who can give you periodic check-ups to see the blind spots in your brand or your business. You might want to encourage feedback from clients, both former and current, who can give you the constructive criticism you need to take your business to a higher level. Or you can enlist the aid of a trusted confidante to ask for feedback. Be sure that person is emotionally detached enough to give you advice that is objective and true, and will help you improve. How will you know when you receive the right advice? By making incremental small adjustments over time, you will always see improvement.

A business leader or person needs to develop a hunger for small adjustments, in the same way a dancer thrives on corrections because they are compliments. The greatest compliment a dancer can hear is, "You've improved." The dancer mindset seeks small adjustments in order to become a better dancer. Too often, businesses and the people who run them get out of control before they think of making a change. Making small adjustments day by day as an ongoing discipline and best business practice is overlooked or ignored. The business must be in trouble and in crisis, losing money or embroiled in scandal, before the need for change is imminent. And then the changes made are so large and sweeping that they undermine the culture, mission, vision and values underlying why the business exists in the first place. It is as if a person went to ballet class every day and performed with incorrect placement, until one day her body suffered a ruptured disk, for which there is no permanent cure.

I have met too many people who have said, *I would like to take a dance class and be a dancer.* These are the people who fail. They do not say, *I would like to take as many dance classes as possible so I can learn to become a dancer.* They want to take the easy way out, and believe that if they take one dance class, they will instantly be a dancer. They do not have the innate understanding of what it takes to be successful at anything! It takes years and years of training to be a dancer, the same way it takes years and years of practice to be good at anything.

We all have blind spots that we cannot recognize on our own. Through dance, I learned to know my daughter in a way I had not known her before. She was now leading me. One Saturday afternoon, we were rehearsing for a piece that was choreographed by Annie de Vuono. I just couldn't hit my marks. I couldn't see where I needed to be on stage—in a window—so the audience would see me. Even though I could not see, Sarah could see where I needed to make adjustments. She was my guide, showing me how I needed to think about where I was moving in relation to her and the other dancers so that at all times I was still visible to the audience. Through dance, our relationship began to change. I was no longer the one in charge. And she knew our relationship was changing. She looked at me and smiled, the way young people do when they have stumbled upon a great truth. She was now a mentor to me. Our relationship was moving in a new direction, the same as the way we moved across the floor. Together, we made many small adjustments.

Training, coaching or mentoring, a good spouse, a good friend, or your children will help you to recognize your blind spots. It is another way of showing that they love you and care about your desire to explore excellence. Left on your own, it is not always possible to recognize your own blind spots. If you practice looking for your own blind spots, you can develop a keen intuition or radar to spot them on your own, but you will never see everything. I have been in ballet classes when world-class dancers who had trained their entire lives were given correction to see the adjustments that they could not see on their own. The experienced dancers' faces flushed with pride. They nodded to the teacher with understanding and gratitude, communicating that they got the correction, by immediately demonstrating the improved movement.

In business, we do not seek enough consistent correction. Financial markets do not correct themselves by making small changes. Instead of making small incremental adjustments, quite often financial markets overcorrect, swinging from one flawed trend to another extreme trend in what I call a *backlash*, also defined as an *overcorrection*. In fact, historically, many businesses often perceive a correction as a negative and hide it from the public. Now, with the advent of the communication age, the new openness, and the emphasis placed on the conversation inherent in all social media, both professionals and businesses have been forced into a state of *constant* correction.

Ballet is an ideal standard. The beauty of ballet inspires you to improve. The discipline and the instruction give you a road map to make small adjustments. In business and in other areas of your life, it is not always easy to see where you need to improve. Many aspects of life are out of our control. We are given certain innate qualities: our appearance, our mannerisms, our personality, our talents, our innate strengths and weaknesses, and our voice. External factors concerning money, health, business and job opportunities can be a matter of pure chance. How well we invest in ourselves, personally or in business (in the financial markets) is always subject to risk and contingent on outside forces.

How can we make small adjustments if we do not know what areas of our lives need to be improved? Life has a funny way of giving you "ballet taps" on your shoulder. If you keep listening and searching, you will clearly see what needs to be changed. Many times, the pattern of what is not working repeats itself. You begin to see a pattern of what is working and what is not.

Actually, making any type of change in business or in life is the greatest challenge of all. Many businesses hire "change consultants," or organizational management consultants, who assess the situation and determine what changes need to be made. Still, both individuals and organizations of all types and sizes often fail to make the change that is needed. The reason why organizations fail is often the same reason why individuals fail. They are not disciplined enough to consistently make the small adjustments that are needed to effect positive change.

By seeking and welcoming correction, we do become better business people. We do build better brands. We also live more enriched lives. You know you are in need of correction, so whom you do ask? A business coach? A business auditing and consulting practice, like McKinsey or Accenture? A trusted friend or colleague? There are professional groups and trade associations, composed of business owners, where you can ask questions and get the kind of feedback that includes the corrections that you need to make.

A word of warning: beware of the coach, consultant or instructor who promises you transformation will be fast, easy and without pain. I was giving a talk in Chicago last year, and an author who does motivational talks and personal growth coaching told me never to tell my audience that something was hard. "These people are over 40," she said, "and they don't want to hear about having to do something hard. Keep things simple. Make it sound easy."

Growth is hard. Building a business is hard. Living is hard. I train in ballet to remind me that all the things in life worth pursuing are hard.

You probably get invitations all the time from well-meaning professionals like the "life coach" in Chicago who offers transformation, inner peace, and accelerated growth—all in a weekend getaway at a retreat center. Achieving transformation, inner peace and growth in a weekend is remarkably ambitious, and feels like a scam to me, sort of like a fat farm for people who are addicted to junk food. Most life coaches, though, do not know how to integrate their physicality with their spiritual wisdom. Some practice yoga a little and can hold a *cobra or plank* position, but I have yet to meet one who can reach for the sky and dance.

If a correction does not resonate with you and you do not feel that you need to make a small adjustment, you can always ask other teachers or consultants for their perspective. You might find that you are not yet able to make the adjustment. So now you must practice, move forward, find ways to make the complete adjustment over time. Try focusing on one correction and working hard every time you train. You will become increasingly dynamic during this process.

Sometimes a correction is wrong! The doctor who gave me advice when I was in my 30s to stop climbing steps was not correct. Twenty-five years later, the rigors of ballet training corrected what had been wrong with my knees. What was needed was the *right* small adjustment.

You must not only accept correction from your instructors and coaches or from life, but you must come to expect it. You must thrive on the chance to improve and to grow. You will develop keen radar for knowing what needs to be corrected. You become your own teacher, your own mentor, your own business coach, and suddenly one day, you are self-correcting your own mistakes long before anyone else sees them. This doesn't mean you can dance or do business in a silo. It only means you have developed the habit of seeking small adjustments as a way to explore your own internal *Barré* of excellence.

When you receive a correction, always smile graciously and thank your teacher, your coach or your consultant. The more corrections you can implement, the more your dance, your life or your business will improve. You have a chance to see how high you can go! How far you can leap? Are your steps fluid, fast and precise? Improvement is a little bit like reaching for heaven and touching the hand of God. Keep going.

For improvement to happen, there are three dance principles that need to be in place.

First, you need to have a clear vision of what you want to achieve. See the ideal image in your head.

Second, you need to break the vision into the small adjustments, or *small, workable tasks* that—over time—will actualize your vision. You must break it down the same way you break down a dance step, in slow motion, so you can see every detail of your footwork. Make a list of what needs to be done, the same way you make a list of all of the dance steps that you need to break down so you can better grasp what needs to be improved.

Third, you must practice at the *Barré* with unerring discipline and devotion, every day, or as often as possible, to make the changes you need in order to actualize your vision. You must do all of the exercises and combinations at the *Barré* that will train your muscles to become the excellent dancer in your vision.

People and organizations fail for three main reasons: They do not have a clear vision. They are unable to break down the vision into small, workable tasks. They are unable to maintain the discipline to implement the small, workable tasks that need to be done every day and sustained over a long period of time.

Why steps? When I was a child, why did steps matter? I guess if you see steps, you want to climb them rather than being stuck at the bottom, wondering what is up at the top. There are many people in this world who do not want to climb steps. It is too hard, too much work, too high, too uncertain; you do not know what awaits you at the top. It may feel safer to stay at the bottom. If you don't try to climb, you never have to worry about feeling the humiliation that can accompany failure. And yet by practicing failure, over time, you learn everything you need to know about exploring excellence. You cannot succeed over the long term without embracing what you have learned through failure. The drive I had to climb steps as a child is the same powerful force that makes me want to dance now.

So why did I begin to dance? Every day, I ask myself this question. At first, I was drawn to dance as an *accidental discovery*. I had been drawn to dance as child, but it was something I never had a chance to do. I don't know why I did not join my high school friend Carmen Canavan and start taking classes with her. Dancing late in life is my destiny. I would not be able to embrace the lessons I learn in dance if I had not already learned about so many other things in life. Martha Graham said, "We learn by practice. Whether it means to learn to dance by practicing dancing or to learn to live by practicing living, the principles are the same. One becomes in some area an athlete of God."

Dancing in its most pure expression is a way to explore the spiritual realm. The practice of ballet makes me feel as though I am reaching for an ideal that is close to God. Going around the circle of the *Rond de Jambé* one more time is the same for me as performing a sacred ritual and reciting a prayer. Religions practice positions, ritual and movement with balletic repetition. The *sign of the cross*, the kneeling on the mat to face Mecca, reaching one's arms in *hallelujah*; there is something powerful about extending one's self far enough to reach for the sky.

"Stealing from the sky" is how Annie de Vuono described where our reach should be while we are doing waltz turns. Sarah and I spent hours in rehearsal for ten weeks. Annie de Vuono choreographed an original piece to a violin concerto by Bach. **Otto Compane, Eight Bells,** was named for the dancers in the piece. In this performance, among the ensemble of eight, my daughter was the youngest dancer and I was the oldest. After training for five years, all of a sudden I could remember whole phrases and combinations. When I first started training, I could not remember three steps, then I progressed to five, then eight. Then I broke through to another level. My body started doing all of the work; the movements were forming fluidly and living in my mind with the certainty of a quiet miracle.

Slowly, incrementally, I was making progress as a dancer, but *my Sarah* was drifting away from me. She was no longer a little girl. One day, she had her hair cut, from the middle of her back to just below her chin. She was growing to be a young woman. On the floor, we moved separately and away from one another. We danced in separate groups and pretended we did not watch one another. We stood at the *Barré* at opposite ends of the studio. We began to separate and become two distinctly different people. She was growing up, and I was giving up a part of myself. I had to let go and give her the most important gift of all—her own space on the floor.

On a cold April day, the ornamental cherry trees were shivering, and shedding petals like pink tears. From the window of PNB's *Studio A*, I leaned against the *Barré* and looked out the window to watch the dance taking place in the trees. It was raining. The wind drove the cherry blossom petals, fluttering like baby butterflies, to the ground. Now the petals lay scattered in mounds of pink snow on the sidewalk.

I had always been a writer, a businesswoman. Actually I have been a lot of things, but a dancer was not one of them. On this particular day, I did not know what I was doing in a ballet class—it was something I would never be very good at doing. One of the hardest things in the world is the prospect of having to do something we are not very good at doing. It's much easier and safer to stick with the things we are moderately proficient in, or to stick with the things we are really good at doing. Since it's my nature to **not** want to do something that I would never be very good at, it's a mystery to me why I found myself in a studio at one of the finest ballet schools in the country, practicing the same steps at the same *Barré*, always pushing myself to pursue a level of excellence that in reality I could not quite achieve. The *ballet ideal* would always elude me.

On that day at PNB, the class was quite full. Many of the students were professional dancers who had years of training behind them. I would never be like them: exquisite dancers, legendary choreographers and magical pianists—there have been too many in my lifetime to mention only a few. I cannot begin to describe what it would be like to have attained the highest level in dance—the pinnacle or the dance ideal. What if I had been handpicked to dance with Baryshnikov or mentored and molded into a dancer by Balanchine?

That day I realized that there was a wide chasm between what the professional dancer has experienced and what I, "a beginning dancer," have come to know about my life through dance. Then I had a startling revelation. Training the way that professional dancers train was giving me the ability to achieve a greater level of excellence in other things that I am good at doing.

Long after my epiphany at PNB, I am still exploring why I train in dance and how it impacts every aspect of my life. Dance has become the outward sign of my passion to live a life full of meaning and purpose. Dance gives a discipline and meaning to my life—a way to embrace the concept of constantly making small, incremental improvements as a full-time metaphysical pursuit. Dance has made me better in business and better in life. Dance makes me feel like I am making a profoundly spiritual connection with all aspects of my life. I am dancing for nothing less than I am reaching for God. I know I may not quite get there, but that will not stop me from reaching.

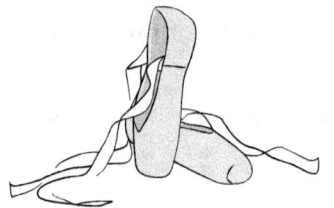

— 4 —

The Four Corners of the Room

The four corners of the room can mean many things. My first impression of a room came from the old brown tenement. The place in the tenement that I claimed as *my room* was actually the stairwell that had steps climbing toward heaven. I lived in my grandmother's tenement for several months while my mother was in the hospital. Although I was only four years old, I had already achieved a certain wisdom. The steps in the tenement were my friends. They gave me the courage to climb.

Every time I climbed the steps, I learned something new about myself. I discovered some strength or came to terms with some hidden weakness. If I prepared for the climb, I could jump up three steps at a time, and sometimes four! I could hop very precisely onto the center of the step. Doing that three times in a row meant my mother would soon be well. If I forgot what I was doing or started thinking about something else, I would stumble.

I found the steps to be a great arbiter of the truth. The steps only praised what was good, excellent and precise in my footwork. I found meaning by climbing the steps. Certain truths prevailed and entered my body, making me see connections and patterns that had little to do with climbing steps and everything to do with life.

My earliest recollection of loving dance was a brief encounter that happened during my teen years. I'd like to say that it was an injury that ended my training, but there is more to the story. While I was playing kickball out on the street, I dislocated my knee and tore cartilage. The doctor didn't consider arthroscopic surgery. He wrapped my knee with a thick Ace bandage and ordered me to use crutches for six weeks. The injury brought my early romance with dance to a halt. During the days I spent on crutches, I thought of no compelling reason beckoning me to dance. There was no teacher at the time like Annie de Vuono, who had the gift to inspire her students to want to become beautiful dancers.

In high school, I loved to accompany my friend Carmen to dance class. In some ways, I believed she was dancing for more than herself. She was also dancing for me and anyone who would watch her. Together, we traveled by subway to a tiny dance studio at Columbus Circle. I was a solitary and shy spectator watching Carmen dance. I sat on a rickety wooden folding chair in the back of the cramped studio. There is a time to be a spectator and there is a time to dance full-out. When I was 17, it was my time to be a spectator, which is ironic, because from a purely physical standpoint, I had all of the right attributes: the speed, agility, and flexibility to be a gifted dancer. But my destiny with dance was yet to unfold.

One of the reasons why people fail in dance, or in business or in life, is because they do not see the four corners of the room and the steps they need to climb. People fail or do not achieve what they want in life or business because they stop short of executing four fundamental characteristics: discipline, focus, flexibility, and perseverance. You have heard these terms wash over you in popular jargon and culture with such frequency that they lose their meaning or impact. Now you can see the terms more concretely, when they are applied to the fundamentals of learning how to dance.

Once I began taking classes, a subtle shift took place. I no longer thought only about my own positioning; I began to develop awareness of my placement relative to the four corners of the room. Even after five years of training, I felt that my change in positioning, turning to face each of the four corners of the room, was barely competent and something I needed to work on.

I like trying different studios and teachers because I always learn something new in technique. Sometimes I am fortunate enough to land in a class that magically emphasizes the exact area I need to work on. One day, right after I was musing to myself about my deficiencies in positioning, I took an open class at PNB with Elaine Bauer. Her style is one of soft-spoken precision; her demeanor is crisp, but elegant. She had us do drills at the *Barré* to help us to improve our positioning. Using our arms, legs and heads, we rotated and turned to face each of the four corners of the room. Elaine commented afterward that ballet was more than training the body; it was also training the mind. Having the experience of this class at just the right time was a small brush with synchronicity. I know that I am doing much more than practicing ballet; I am training my mind to explore excellence.

Beyond the physical space of knowing where my body stood and how it moved relative to my placement at the *Barré* or on the floor, I realized that the four corners of the room were highly symbolic of the four principles in ballet and in life, as well as in branding and business. These four principles that always need to work in unison are: *discipline, focus, flexibility, and perseverance.*

— DISCIPLINE —

People fail in life or in business for many reasons, some of which are out of any one person's control. People get sick or are obligated to take care of loved ones. There are real obstacles blocking your actualization such as illnesses, dying, death, accidents, bad timing and bad luck. You can't control the cards that life deals to you, but you can control how well you play the hand that you have been given. A primary reason why people fail to live their lives well or to build their businesses is because they don't understand all the hard work that is required to achieve a higher level of performance. And there is also a complete unawareness about how this hard work must be done day-in, day-out, indefinitely, over a long period of time. Usually forever.

There are no *paid* vacation days when you are committed to the ideal of exploring excellence. Take time off and it is at your own risk. More often than not, the real risk is, the longer the break you take from discipline, the harder it is to get back in shape again.

When the amazing prima ballerina Gelsey Kirkland was asked what life lessons ballet has taught to her, she responded, "That the necessity in ballet to apply strict boundaries in order to attain freedom can be a starting point for finding a similar truth in everyday life."*

Keep in mind that one of the greatest business minds of all times, Peter Drucker, once said, "Hard work, including physical fitness, isn't a prescription with universal appeal. But it's inescapable." It is not surprising at all how a great ballerina and a great business leader would be in alignment regarding the concept of discipline.

Professional ballet dancers rarely miss a technique class or a rehearsal because as soon as you start missing classes, you start losing your form and precision. Even when dancers are downed by illness or injury, they find a dozen ways to keep training in order to keep their muscles in peak condition. I am

---

* Straight from the heart: Gelsey Kirkland looks back... and ahead Dance Magazine, Sept. 2005 by Kate Lydon

a far cry from being a professional dancer and yet, despite my busy schedule, I will always manage to squeeze a ballet class into my workday. Even when I travel, I make the time to dance.

When I first began training in dance, the changes taking place inside of me were mostly physical. For adults who choose to train in dance, you will see changes occur in every part of your body. Ballet strengthens and tones every muscle group, and works on developing some tiny or "rapid-twitch" muscles that over time will improve your ability to rise higher.

Hips, thighs and legs. You will begin to see muscles develop in your legs that you never knew existed. You will see sculpted definition in your inner thighs and calves. Your outer hips will turn out and gain strength that will emanate up through your spine and cause you to stand more erect and cause you to feel like you are physically rising higher.

Abdominals, back and neck. Your body core is the entire area around your pelvis and abdomen. Through training, your core will strengthen so that the muscles in your back, hips and abdomen work together to form your posture, shooting up through your spine to your neck, and ultimately support your head.

Shoulders, arms and upper torso. Ballet arms are used for balance, artistic expression and development of the *ligne*. Your arms and shoulders will increase in tone and strength but not develop a visible muscularity. If you are after *cuts*, you will have to take up weightlifting at the gym to gain more solid definition. In early training, one of the most challenging things to is learn how to gracefully extend your arms to their full reach without pulling up or clenching your shoulders.

The derriere. All athletic strength comes from the great gluteus maximus. You will see your gluteus develop orb-like and round, rising higher, unlike the flattened behinds of the great masses of the unexercised, or the pulverized bottoms of those who have been liposuctioned or implanted with bulbous silicone.

During my passage through the change-of-life, I put on weight and developed a thickening in the middle for no good reason. I was obviously training and eating well, but I was stubborn. I wanted my youthful shape back through hard work and discipline. For years I had a client who was a plastic surgeon, and I could see him eyeing my thickening waist as if I should get on with it and "get hosed." I used to joke with him that if I had the fat liposuctioned, it would only return to my brain. There is no compelling argument for getting liposuction. If you have extra fat, it is there for a reason and it is best to deal with the cause. If you rid yourself of the outward sign, you do not eliminate the reason for the fat. There are many thin people (the skinny obese) who have dangerously high cholesterol, because even though they have been cosmetically altered, they have not dealt with the root cause of their fat—poor eating habits and lack of exercise. It took time and many hours of hard work, but my body shape did return to its youthful shape. It is not a bad place, at all, to be a woman of a certain age who can still wear *the bikini*.

The chief arbiter of the ballet class is the mirror. At first, you do not want to see the mirror. You do not want to see yourself, moving or not moving, as you really are. The mirror does not lie. I know I am getting older. And, truth be told, what is so bad about getting older? Despite the advancing years, every now and then when I catch a glimpse of myself in the mirror, I am amazed to see a body that has shaved years off of its chronological age. My body is surprisingly lithe, taut and shapely. Ballet hasn't turned back the clock, but it has put up a wondrous fight against gravity. Women who consistently train in ballet just can't seem to form saddlebags, jiggle thighs, lumpy midsections, and flat saggy butts.

Sue is in her early 70s and attends the morning open classes at Pacific Northwest Ballet (PNB). She hasn't had a lot of dance training and cannot do turns and the long, complicated *adagio* or *grande allegro* sequences, but she always completes her training at the *Barré*. During the floor work she mimics the steps in small, amended movements. Her posture is strong. Her legs are limber and well-developed. For a woman in her 70s, her body looks to be 20 years younger.

During my last visit to Steps on Broadway, Emilietta Ettlin pranced around the floor with the lithe movement of a 16-year-old girl instead of a 60-year-old woman. After the *Barré*, I did Pilates-style exercises on the floor. I reclined in prone position and did sharp scissor kicks. Emilietta came over to me and adjusted my position, forcing me to sit up higher and to kick more dagger-like, while maintaining my bottom like a perfectly balanced bowl on the floor. Then she looked deeply into my eyes and said, "This one small adjustment will change your life."

Swiss-born Emilietta Ettlin has danced with major companies in Europe and America, and has been coached in ballets by great choreographers such as Edward Villella and Melissa Hayden. She developed her own *ballet floor technique* when she was a professional dancer. Once when she was injured for five months, she was only able to do her own *ballet floor technique*. She returned from the injury stronger and was able to do higher extensions.

As I learned to dance, over time I began to see more clearly that so many of our mishaps, catastrophes, broken dreams, and false starts in life are due to our refusal to do the hard work that is required to explore excellence. Striving for any ideal, noble or not, striving for anything you want to attain in life, requires nothing less than giving it *your all*. Sacrifice and hard work must always be sustained over time to achieve a higher level of performance.

In a rare press interview, actress Shirley MacLaine described her work ethic as being derived from years and years of the discipline of dance training: "I have a work ethic that never quits. I'm basically a team player. I'm never late. I once missed a performance; I had a temperature of 106. But I've performed with a fever of 104, and going offstage in between numbers to throw up. I think I was just trained."*

In the business world, having a good professional reputation is obviously connected to establishing one's brand identity, but many people don't think about the discipline that is required to nurture this identity. Like ballet training, your reputation is carefully cultivated and trained over time. It does not happen by accident. Your reputation or professional brand is established by doing the same things repeatedly over time, whether you feel like doing them or not. Brand fitness requires the same level of focused discipline as the physical fitness required in ballet training and must be exercised on a regular schedule.

When I first walked into a ballet class during that Saturday afternoon in September, I didn't know how to place my feet in first position. I only had three things going for me: I had the desire to show up for class, the ability to pay for lessons, and as Annie de Vuono pointed out, I had great feet. The first desire, to show up for class, quickly expanded to showing up for class on time.

Anyone who has ever taken a dance class knows how embarrassing it is to arrive late after the class has begun, and feel the stony stare of everyone's eyes while you fumble to find a place at the *Barré*. Inevitably, if you are late for a class, it is the day that all the places are taken. You wander through the room trying to appear at once invisible and at the same time hopeful that someone will move to offer you a space. Most of the time no one will make room at the *Barré* , and you must wedge in between two

---

* Shirley MacLaine On Life, Showbiz and Finding Contentment
By Moira Macdonald Seattle Times June 12, 2010 http://seattletimes.nwsource.com/html/movies/2012073537_shirley13.html

closely spaced bodies who now seem bent on kicking you in the head before the *grand battement*.* Ballet, like business, can be a ruthless and competitive *brand milieu*.

If you take any warm body on the planet and send it to daily ballet training, no matter the level of raw physical talent, or lack thereof, the body-in-training will begin to show improvement. By showing up and doing, over time there will be progression just from the sheer repetition of the movement. Every *Barré* has a series of exercises and works in the *tendu*, the *degagé*, the *Rond de Jambé* and the *grand battement*, among numerous others. Doing it, day-in and day-out, whether you want to or not, is the discipline that results in improvement.

John Hanes (not his real name) lives in Lacey, Washington, and works for a small state government agency. Every Saturday, John drives 90 minutes from Lacey to Seattle to take dance at the PNB. As a dancer, he is not particularly gifted. John is pushing 60 and does not have a classic ballet body. He is overweight, with a top-heavy torso, a bulbous-shaped head, no neck, and forearms like Popeye. But in three years, I have seen him improve dramatically. Now he no longer lumbers around the room, and when he waltzes across the floor, it is with some measure of fluidity.

An even more dramatic story about discipline and dance is Gregg Mozgala, a 32-year-old actor with cerebral palsy. Cerebral palsy is a degenerative disease that causes the brain to misfire so that the muscles do not receive the signals needed to control movement.**

---

* Every *Barré* includes the grand battement exercise where the working leg is raised from the hip into the air and brought down again. For the neophyte grand battement requires high but controlled kicks with straight legs, pointed toes and a torso that remains still and centered.
** Learning His Body, Learning to Dance by NEIL GENZLINGER, NYT November 25, 2009 http://www.nytimes.com/2009/11/25/arts/dance/25palsy.html?pagewanted=all

A story about Gregg Mozgala in the *New York Times* describes how, through dance training, he changed the way he walks. Mozgala said that for most of his life, he walked up on his toes, and wobbled from side to side to maintain balance. Mozgala teamed with a choreographer, Tamar Rogoff, who created a piece for him called "Diagnosis of a Faun." It premiered at La MaMa Annex in the East Village of New York City.

Ms. Rogoff stated in the *New York Times*, "I didn't know what I was going to do for him," she said, "but I just knew he was inspiring to me." Prior to working with Gregg Mozgala, she did not study cerebral palsy because she did not want to develop a biased opinion about what could be done or not done. Instead, she created a physical regimen to retrain his body beyond the narrow ken of the locked-in *cerebral palsy* patterns of movement that were developed over time.

As Mr. Mozgala changed, so did Ms. Rogoff's concept for the dance. He was able to accomplish more in eight months of dance training than he had experienced during twelve years of physical therapy. Ms. Rogoff calls Mr. Mozgala "the best student I've ever had." Both are intensely focused on what is next for Mr. Mozgala, who knows that dance is not a cure. For years, everyone had told him there was nothing he could do to improve, but Ms. Rogoff gave him an option. "It's not over," he said. "There's always a chance to change. You should not—you dare not—give up."

When I first showed up in ballet class, my spine was curving inward and I had developed a swayback. *Lordosis* is the medical term used to describe the inward curvature of a portion of the spine. One of the possible causes of a swayback is osteoporosis, which runs in my family. My mother suffered from it, and so did my grandmother. What I recall more than anything was the gradual process of the condition. A massage therapist said to me one day, "Do you know that you have a curvature in your spine?" I could see it happening, but it wasn't so dramatic. Not at first.

It took five years of constant training before my back became straight. Some of my teachers emphasized my posture in my training more than others. At PNB, Alexandra Dickson corrected me in every class so often that she could just say my name and I automatically knew to take my pelvis and tilt down. Over time, in every *plié, demi* or *grande*, I could see the curve lessening and my back expanding to be straight and strong.

Conversely, I have seen people walk into ballet class and believe they should be able to do things easily, just because they showed up. My Sarah is a marvelous athlete with a fantastic ballet body, and yet she cannot beat her feet fast to do *frappes or the little beats (petite battements sur le coup-de-pied)*. She has not yet trained enough to develop the little rapid-twitch muscles that will give her feet speed and precision. Her insistence on expecting instant results is a sign of her inexperience and youth, similar to business people who want overnight success without putting in the hard work to build brands.

Twyla Tharp said, "Dance has never been a particularly easy life, and everybody knows that." And yet in my life—apart and separate from the dance world—I have known many people who think dancing is easy. All you have to do is take a class or two, they suppose.

— FOCUS —

I don't think anyone can teach you how to focus. I think focus is one of those things that takes training. You learn by practice. You learn by doing.

Once I started taking dance, and even in spite of my physical limitations—age, bad knees, and lordosis—the bug bit me and I was determined to be the best I could be. In my wildest fantasies, I was dancing around doing triple turns and leaping across the floor in perfect *grand jetés* and landing so softly that my feet gently grazed the floor without making a sound. No matter what, I would try to reach the ideal even if I knew in all my rational thought that truly excellent performance would always elude me. As my teacher Annie de Vuono always said, "The dancer in my head is just excellent."

When I'm in the moment and training at the *Barré* or on the floor, I can't think of my limitations. In a funny way, I can't even focus on a goal for the class, because the improvements that are made are so small and so incremental; they cannot always be seen or even felt. The day-in, day-out training is like implementing tactics in business. You keep focus by doing small things every day that accumulate and build up over time, to the point where all of a sudden, something big happens and you see lasting results.

I never walked into a ballet class and said, today is the day I will finally be able to do a *pirouette*. One day I just turned, and it happened. And then in the next class, it didn't happen. Then six months later, I would be able to do a *pirouette* more often than not. Then in another year, I could do a *pirouette* every time, but not all of them would be good. I will be working on these *pirouettes* for as long as I am able to train in ballet. Multiples? I would like to do triples next year. And I don't know if a time will come when all of my *pirouettes* will be great. But the dancer in my head can do anything.

In every class, I can only focus on being completely mentally present and knowing where my positioning is on the floor. I need to know where my body is at all times and in relation to the other dancers, who are moving all around me. I need to know my precise placement as my space shifts while we are moving together across the floor. I need to give dance all of me. It is one of the few experiences in which I am completely into myself and yet at the same time I am completely out of myself.

This level of focus is the same as *Zen* or *being in the zone*. I have no choice but to do my best work. And by doing my best work, I am doing all of the little things that will accumulate over time and get powerful results.

Ballet works and develops many small and seemingly hidden muscles, but the most important muscle of all to train is your brain. You can focus and reconfigure your brain. Amazing. The level of intense focus is the same, if not more intense, as yoga. Yoga requires positioning, but essentially you stay in one place on your mat. While yoga requires infinite focus, you do not have to be moving around a room full of other dancers who are also moving. Ballet is more than training and discipline; it is time to quiet the mind and to meditate on the fact that nothing in the world matters except what you are doing. You are dancing. You are here and now, where dance lives and endures for all time. The same level of focus applies when you are training your brain to do all of those small tasks to build a professional brand and to build a business. Without interruption, without distraction, your solid focus is only on what you are doing. You have given all of yourself to be in the moment.

— FLEXIBILITY —

Why do I have great feet? Ask a ballet teacher. I don't know, but I believe it may be I have very high arches and my toes are relatively even in length, not too short or too long. My ankles are strong. My body is strong and supple. I am flexible and can stretch deeply. I had always been physically fit and exercised daily, but ballet is much more demanding and all encompassing. Through ballet, you endure a complete range of training and become aware of your entire body in exacting detail.

Flexibility is much more than a set of physical attributes. Flexibility is a state of mind. It means that despite all of your discipline and the many ways you practice and train over time, you must constantly be on the lookout to see when something you are doing is not working and when you need to make a change. It's like looking at your business and seeing every component: what works, what doesn't work, what areas need to be improved immediately and what areas can only be improved over time. The greatest challenge of all is the ability to maintain discipline while being observant enough to identify what needs to be changed.

Physically speaking, flexibility is both learned and genetic. Everyone is born with a certain range of flexibility. Consistent training will enhance and refine your natural flexibility. And lack of consistent training will make you lose flexibility.

Denise is a mom; she has a desk job in an office. On occasion, she dances, but not frequently enough to stay in shape. Over the past four years, since her pregnancy, she lost nearly all of her turnout and now has a less-than-90-degree turnout in first position. She finds she cannot stand in first position without clenching her quads and gluteus muscles. Once in a blue moon, I see her in a class. She wants to know if there is some kind of exercise that she can do during the work day that will help her regain some of her flexibility and strength in her turnout.

I don't know what Denise does for a living and I don't know what she stands for. She complains about the inflexibility of her job. She may be weak in her turnout and want to know the quick and easy way to regain her muscle tone. But there is no substitute for doing the hard work she needs to do to build her muscle. Denise's job may be inflexible, but she is not doing the hard work and putting in the time that she needs to do to get herself a flexible position.

I have taken a few ballet floor *Barré* classes that are designed to accelerate learning technique. Zena Rommett developed a floor *Barré*, which is taught frequently at Steps on Broadway in New York. Another floor *Barré* is taught by Emilietta Ettlin at Steps, where she trains students to use the resistance of the floor and emphasizes the use of the inner thigh to prevent the over-development of the upper thigh. This technique helps the student find correct placement in the rotation of the leg in the hip socket to maximize turnout.

Ettlin advises dancers to warm up before the first class of the day, and especially before stretching. "The warm-up period should last fifteen minutes for those under thirty years of age, and thirty minutes for those over age thirty." The older you are, the longer period of time you should take to warm up. In fact, you should never stop moving. "Most dancers do not understand," said Ettlin, "that injuries can be caused by weaknesses in muscles that cannot do what is demanded of them."

Your business also has many muscles that must be worked out systematically to make the entire business successful and prosperous. Otherwise, it can be damaged by the weaknesses in certain areas that cannot integrate with the whole business.*

Flexibility must be exercised in every part of your body: Your toes, ankles, knees, thighs, hamstrings, hip, pelvis, lower back, derriere, neck and shoulders. And while much is made of these individual parts of the body, it is the total integration of all the parts working together organically that trains a body to become a well-toned ballet body. Flexibility has to be practiced every day. If you don't use it, you lose it.

Brand flexibility requires the same level of focused discipline as physical fitness and must be exercised on a regular schedule. Your brand has to be stretched, loosened up and taken for a walk. You need to run your brand the same way you run your body. In the same way, it is necessary to do many things to build

---

* Quotes attributed to Emilietta Ettlin from **Stretch and Strengthen** by Judy Alter, Houghton Mifflin Company, 2 Park Street, Boston, MA 02108.

your brand and build your business; all of the different parts must work together organically. You must do many things to build your reputation and your business.

— PERSEVERANCE —

After I walked into Annie de Vuono's class, it took two years of training, for three-to-five classes a week, at Belltown Ballet's beginning classes before I could take Annie's class on a regular basis. You see, I had unwittingly walked into her intermediate class, which requires students to have several years of training. It is not uncommon for the adult beginning dancer to stay in a beginning ballet class for several years or even for the rest of one's life. It's not easy for the adult dancer to master ballet. The level of synovial fluid in one's joints diminishes, and flexibility is not always sinewy and limber.

The most difficult part of training as an adult dancer is that you don't have the archival dance memory—your body has the *history of knowing* how to put steps together to create a fluid movement. Even after five years of training, I would find myself waltzing across the floor and then completely blank out and forget the next steps. Annie de Vuono always says, "When you're training as an adult dancer, you just have to get the steps into your body."

Every dancer who is first learning must have a mentor, someone who knows the steps better than you do, to follow on the floor. I remember a beautiful dancer, "*Maria*." With her long braid down to the middle of her back, her large brown eyes and sinewy limbs, she dances skillfully and passionately. *Maria* is my guide. No matter where I go, in every class, I have always found my "*Maria*," my muse, who knows the steps better than I do By following *Maria*, I am getting the steps into my own body so that I can eventually own the steps for myself.

I always say in jest that it has taken me many ballet classes to be able to dance this poorly. As an adult-in-training, the greatest number of classes I have ever taken in a week is six. If I was a young ballet professional, maybe I could take several classes a day. On the days I don't take ballet, I cross-train. I take Pilates or I ride the stationary bike, lift weights for upper body or walk a couple of miles. I like to take Kari Anderson's "Reach" class on Sunday night at *Pro-Robics*, which is a combo of ballet training and Pilates, with a touch of yoga. It is true core strength and balance training. One Sunday when Kari was demonstrating a complicated move, she said, "Don't worry about getting it right now; you have a whole lifetime to make it perfect." I like her way of thinking, and it spills over into everything in my life and in my business.

When someone new comes into a class I'm taking, I can tell if they have had any training, or if they are taking the same first steps that I took when I walked into Annie de Vuono's class wearing my stiff ballet slippers. And my heart goes out to them, because I want them to stay. If you find the right teacher, you will stay.

The four corners of the room are also the four internal spaces we need to visit every day. Akin to the Hindu tradition, you must visit four realms: the physical, the mental, the emotional and the spiritual. There is complete artistic freedom and reward when you do the work in each space to achieve your center, your core strength and your balance. As Martha Graham said, "There is vitality, a life force, energy, a quickening, that is translated through you into action, and because there is only one of you in all time, this expression is unique."

No matter how many times you take a step, or are confident in the ones you have taken, you can never stop; you must take many more. This past January, I took an open ballet class at PNB with Bruce Wells. I have taken his class many times before. I like his verbal style of teaching. He doesn't demonstrate steps; he calls them out, one step at a time, a string of French phrases for an entire combination.

The class was in the large studio C, where the corps rehearses their performances. So the majority of the students in this big class were professionals—members of the corps who were on break after the long, grueling *Nutcracker* season. Only a fraction of the dancers were adults like me—newcomers and late bloomers, the hobbyists—who just happen to love training in dance. The floor work was difficult for me. My body doesn't have a "dance history" to draw upon, so it can't just take over and perform, the way it would if I had trained as a child.

Every combination was so fast! I felt like I was traveling down a freeway and speeding, overdriving my headlights, not knowing where I was going, just to stay up with the traffic flow. I am only grateful that I didn't crash! It was really hard, and I do not know why I stayed for the last two combinations. Sheer persistence. Strength. Endurance. These qualities are very attractive to me and have served me well in business, but I'm not sure about ballet. Was I brave to get out on the floor and dance badly among so many people who could dance so well? I do not know. And I do not know if I improved my technique at all. Only time will tell.

Dance demands your total engagement. I do know that the power of focus is with me, like both a magical elixir and also a springboard for doing all the things that seem impossible or completely out of reach. The only way to learn focus is to practice it as a discipline. You can think more about discipline, focus, flexibility and perseverance, but more than that, always remember your passion.

Annie de Vuono is famous for giving her students a difficult combination to do and announcing, "Let's crush this sucker."

Sarah and I trained through grueling rehearsals for Annie's piece, *Otto Compane*. Annie made us run through the routine once, then twice, then three more times. Five more times. We were in technical mode—doing the steps, getting the steps down. Each time we ran through the piece, Annie emphasized a different aspect of how we are moving. During one run-through, the focus was on our arms, arms, arms. We were walking around the room, holding our arms fully extended in second position, like the spreading wings of large birds or airplanes. Then the next practice, we focused on our breath. Another run-through focused on the generosity we are giving to the audience—here we were doing more than dancing. We were feeling the movement. We were giving ourselves over wholly to the piece. Marlo Martin, the owner of eXitSPACE, came in and watched us and asked us to find the joy in Annie's piece. Two more run-throughs, then we were done. We crushed the sucker, at least for the day.

I looked out the window to the street and snow was blowing in the wind. It was too gentle to be real snow and had a dance of its own. Pale pink petals were falling from cherry trees. I turned to my daughter and saw her beauty in a way I had not seen her before. She had always been a girl and now she had turned into a young woman I barely recognized, almost overnight, it seemed. When had this young girl, my daughter, become a woman? From across the room, I was seeing her as a woman for the first time. She, too, was looking out the window, watching the petals swirling in the air. One day, I will look back and remember the dance of the pink snow. Sadness, beauty, profound joy, dance is all of these things—and so is watching my little girl go away so this young woman can take her place.

After I leave a ballet class, I experience these amazing moments. Some days, I shed soft little tears because I cannot get a single step. And each step seems so difficult; I do not think I will ever get it. There is the looming reality that for every year I train, I am also growing another year older. I know no matter how much time I spend training, my chronological age is seeping into my bones and petrifying like wood in a proud but stubborn old oak tree. And yet by working hard and by putting in the time, through sheer will and discipline, I make these tiny, incremental improvements, like baby steps. After taking hundreds of dance classes, some days I cry a little because suddenly I get a step that I never thought I would be able to do.

— 5 —

Rising Higher

I feel a sense of longing when I remember the New York tenement that was home to my childhood steps. I don't think the old brown tenement should have been abandoned. Left vacant, someone torched the building. Had it not been abandoned, it would not have burned to the ground. The fire was caused by arson, but never investigated. Case closed. Soon after the fire, the old people who lived in the other brownstones on the block were pushed out. The developers came and paved the way for a new low-income, ghetto apartment project; people would get welfare vouchers to live there.

Someone made a profit by razing the old tenement. I can't name names. I'm not in the habit of knowing unscrupulous developers and politicians. I am willing to bet, none of them knew how to dance.

During the time when the tenement was destroyed, I was living far away, on the West coast, so I do not know exactly what happened. I do know it made no sense for my grandmother Katherine to walk away from the home where she had lived for 40 years. But we're not talking about sense. The Sheedy folk, Katherine's in-laws, had a reputation for lacking the knowledge of worldly realities. Someone had talked Katherine into believing that she really didn't own the tenement where she had lived for so long. Katherine lived in the house long after her husband

Dick Sheedy had died. The house was owned free and clear, but Katherine didn't have a deed.

There was a story of a feud between my Grandfather Dick Sheedy and his brother John Sheedy, both of whom wanted the house, but neither of whom could produce the original deed of trust. The feud started in the 1930s, and never grew heated or nasty, but neither brother ever made up. There were a lot of Irish wakes and weddings where they sat side-by-side, stony-faced, sometimes drunk, sometimes cold sober, neither one ever saying one word to the other. Just one of those situations Irish families are famous for.

For all those years, my grandparents had to be paying taxes on the tenement. Not having a deed is no reason not to pay taxes. The government is not known to overlook people or properties that don't pay taxes. For those of us who know a little about law, paying taxes on a property for over 40 years certainly constitutes legal ownership.

Dick and Katherine Sheedy's oldest daughter, my Aunt Dolly, let the tenement go. Dolly moved my grandmother into an assisted living community and walked away. She took most of Katherine's belongings to the city dump and said there was no legal claim to the tenement. Katherine didn't have a deed. No one had a deed, not even a bank. But to get Katherine to move out, I think someone did a deal behind closed doors. Someone took money for the tenement and no one said a thing. Everyone is dead now, so there is no telling what kind of deal was done.

I return often to New York City on business, but I rarely visit my hometown, Yonkers. I don't usually let anyone know I am there. It's not like anyone would care or expect me to drop in. No one is there any more. The family has long fragmented and people are strewn everywhere, like broken pieces of china. The Sheedy family is a cracked heirloom that no one thinks of trying to glue together because it was never really whole in the first place. This is a family composed of introverts who are madcap, some certifiably so, loners, often engaged in solitary pursuits. When they reach out for a human connection, it is not because they need to; it is because they are extending a sincere offering to share a bit of their time with you. There is no pretense among these people. There is no sense that something is owed or there is an obligation. These are people who only speak from the heart or they will not speak at all.

There is more to the story of the old brown tenement than I can say before we return to **Steps**. My Sarah has never met anyone from the Sheedy clan; they were all long gone before her time. Everywhere I go, and everywhere I take a dance class, I think of Sarah, and long for her to be beside me. We have a special way of connecting with one another on the dance floor that we do not have in our ordinary day-to-day lives. We are mother and daughter, and yet we are turning together in time, transcending the here and now and doing something extraordinary together. At the same time, we are drifting apart. Sarah is becoming her own person and I am letting go. She is learning to define the outer edges of who she is becoming. She has no choice but to leave her mother behind. She does intuitively understand the power of climbing steps. The only way you can climb steps is if you stand on your own two feet.

One day, on the way to dance class, Sarah told me that she is feeling intense uncertainty about the world. Her uneasiness is based on something much more than the fact that she is a senior about to graduate from high school. Sarah is prescient. When I was pregnant with her, I had a premonition that she was the one who was going to be the most like me—and sure enough, she has the gift of prescience. We talk about the changing world and the paradigm shifts taking place on many fronts. Too many meltdowns to name. The media has become completely fragmented. Wars are raging in Iraq and Afghanistan. We know energy is changing—oil and gas are in their final death throes. We know major climate changes are happening and food shortages will increase. Nuclear meltdown is happening in Japan. Joblessness, inflation, foreclosures, banks, currency—the financial markets are re-setting. The new homeless are everywhere.

And yet, we are training to be dancers, and like cats, we will always land on our feet. We drive on, passing runners, joggers, baby carriages, people walking dogs under the hazy fall of pink snow.

Then I was off to New York City. Late June brought intense heat and humidity that was more than a hint of summer. In the evenings, I sat in the little park in Tudor City, looking at the tall brown stalks, remnants of the tulips that had proudly bloomed in May. I was back in New York on business, but more importantly, it was my third year of ballet training, taking non-stop classes. I was kind of like an old tulip stalk that had shed its colorful bloom, but it did not matter. I always have this idea that my mission in life is to rise higher. It is not only my mission; I have decided that is why we are all here on earth. Our greatest moments of courage are found when we choose to rise higher.

In New York City, I took ballet classes at Steps on Broadway. It was an easy commute from midtown, a quick jaunt to the shuttle and to the No. 1 train up to 72nd Street. Steps offers many dance classes every day and through the years, I have trained with a wide range of teachers. Gelsey Kirkland taught an advanced class at Steps. I longed to take a class with her, and not because I had any illusions that I could keep up. If I had been training in ballet for three years and I was only twelve, I would still not be ready to take an advanced class with Gelsey Kirkland. After three years of training as an adult, my only focus was on rising higher.

The next day was Saturday. I started the morning by taking

a ballet class with Robert Atwood. I thought it was a good way to warm up and prepare for the advanced class.

After class, I lingered in the lobby and waited for a time. I felt unsure of myself. I wondered what it would be like to see this phenomenal ballerina, Gelsey Kirkland, in real life. Moments before the class was about to begin, I saw a petite woman climbing up the steps in the stairwell. The steps were metal, like the steps in a tenement, and her footsteps echoed in the hallway. Tiny, she wore her brown hair in a long braid that cascaded down her back. Her sweatshirt was baggy, and large dark sunglasses dominated her face. It was a powerful moment for me to realize that the first time I laid eyes on this remarkable dancer, she too was climbing her own steps.

I greeted her warmly and asked her if it was okay if I took her class, even though I was not an advanced student. She nodded her head with understanding and said, "Do whatever you can do. Do the best you can do."

The class was like any other, except this time I was in the same room with Gelsey Kirkland, one of the most extraordinary ballerinas of our time. She repeated affirmations to her students, frequently commenting *"good job"* or *"good work,"* as if it was important to remind ourselves that ballet is never easy, but after years of hard work, devotion and training it should look as if it is the easiest thing in the world for anyone to do.

Dance demands a lightness of being and the special quality of appearing to float in the air. It is no wonder so many dancers are lithe and sinewy, almost approaching professional model standards of thinness. It appears to be aesthetics on the one hand, which is true, but also there are fewer pounds of pressure coming down on the floor, which means less stress and impact on your joints, bones, ligaments, and tendons.

Classical dance training is a high-intensity workout that will increase your muscle strength and your stamina. You will find that your reflexes quicken so that you can spring into action. Your balance stabilizes so that you can sustain any action you undertake. To rise higher, you will want to develop a physical discipline, whether ballet or something else, in the same way that you want to develop the grace, elegance and strength of who you are as a person.

The physicality of ballet training sounds trite and superficial when you consider how it is affecting your mind, your very being. Back to the mirror image. You want to see the line of your body in the mirror. You also want to feel the alignment of your whole personhood—who you really are. You want to feel your innate core strength. Now, standing there before the mirror, you know who you really are and you know who you are not. The ultimate mission of ballet training is for you to develop the deepest possible awareness of yourself. This self-awareness is far more than physicality and touches upon the core of your being—the inner workings of your soul. Through the discipline of training, you are outside yourself, on a higher plane, a spiritual plane, where your physicality has taken you. One doesn't get to be spiritual just by thinking about it. You have to do something tangible and physical to get there.

I love the metaphorical power of the *Barré*—doing the same thing over and over, seeing a change, sometimes a small change or hardly any change. But one thing I know for certain is that I am there to test the limits of the *Barré*. My ability to focus on the *Barré*, metaphorically speaking, gives me a retreat from a world that is not always kind, and even more harsh than I care to discuss. My focus on the *Barré* gives me additional strength to withstand any adversity that I encounter.

Alexandra Dickson from PNB said, "With *grand pliés*, it is not how far down you go. What matters most is to rise as high as you can reach." No matter what happens, real-life tragedies, setbacks, failures and disappointments, you do not have to stay down. We all travel through the muck and mire that threatens to weigh us down. The discipline in **Steps** is to reach, one step at a time, taking multiple steps, and whenever possible to appear as we are leaping over many steps that have melded together, in a single fluid movement.

Rise higher even when you are going down. One of the most basic ballet positions is doing a *grand plié*. Even as you bend your knees deeply, you are still holding your upper body erect and rising higher. What you are doing is graceful, and one step higher toward reaching for the embodiment of beauty. Rising higher even as you are going down is a metaphor for every aspect of your life. It means even when everything is going to hell, you are still seeking a way to take the high road out of the storm and into the sun.

Ballet can help you do what is seemingly impossible. Barbara Willis has danced since she was a child. As she approached her 60s, it became difficult for her to use her hands, even to do simple things such as writing a letter. She consulted a neurologist and found out that she had Parkinson's disease. Soon she found that by practicing movement, she was better able to manage the symptoms of her disease and keep them at bay. Her balance was stronger, her posture stayed erect, and her movements were smoother. She took her experience as a dancer and created a class, held at Spectrum Wellness and Rehabilitation Center in Colorado Springs, Colorado, to help others who have this disease. "Parkinson's wants to take you and fold you in half and never let you go," Willis says. She describes the power of dance as "Every move is a way to slowly unfold again."*

In every ballet class, I discover some nuance I must work on. There is some little thing I have been doing the wrong

---

* Controlled Moves Sun Journal June 28 2009
http://www.newbernsj.com/articles/disease-46186-parkinson-willis.html

way, but that is what put me on the road to explore excellence. Eventually, I will discover the correction that needs to be made. It is through this process that I am continually in a state of rising higher. According to Martha Graham, "Practice means to perform, over and over again in the face of all obstacles, some act of vision, of faith, of desire. Practice is a means of inviting the perfection desired."

Each time I go back to ballet class, I realize I must learn how to walk again because one more class is one more step in transforming how I move. Walking is also called ambulation. It is one of the chief characteristics of being human. You walk upright on two legs. Walking is often defined as locomotion of the upper body being carried along by the lower body's limbs.

Dancers walk differently from those who do not dance. Their turnout is apparent in their gait. You can see their hips rotating out. Backs straight. Heads held high. There is a certain postural distinction. I interviewed the choreographer James Canfield, who said, "When I first meet the dancers, I have the dancers walk for me. I turn on the music, and then I ask the dancers to let me see them move—that is my jumping off."

One time I was on the upper west side of Manhattan on my way to Steps on Broadway to take a dance class. I saw Gelsey Kirkland striding down 72nd Street in perfect fourth position. She wasn't merely walking; it was as if she was gliding forward, with the long strides of someone who was on a march ever upward and pointing toward heaven.

Since you are human, you probably only have two legs working for you. Try not having a leg or two. You might not be able to dance—unless you are Challes Reese, a teenage girl with cerebral palsy who dances across a stage in a wheelchair. Challes became the first student who used a wheelchair to perform in the annual Iowa State Dance and Drill Team Association competition. The ability to express what is at the core of one's soul through the language of dance transcends human limitations. With dance, anything is possible.*

One night, I had a dream about my son David. His hair is long and curly, the way it was when he used to visit me. He was 18 and dating a girl named *India*. He is smiling and placid; the expression on his face is almost cherubic. He is at peace with what is going on with his illness, and he has achieved a new level of fulfillment. His foot has healed; he is able to run again. I want him to know that anything is possible. If I can dance the way I do, he too can rise higher.

I told my son that I have been plagued with bad dreams and that I worry about him. He said, "At least you wake up. At least they are not real." There was an article in today's *New York Times* about how difficult it has been to try to identify the gene sequence that caused his illness; it is a more rare sequence or cluster than was originally suspected. My mother. My son.

The remarkable dancer and dance educator Timothy Lynch told me a story—he was teaching in an elementary school. One young boy was autistic and did not join the rehearsals; he would not dance. After much encouragement, the teacher told Tim that the boy was not going to participate.

The autistic boy stayed on the sidelines, seemingly oblivious to all the other kids in the class, who were dancing. Weeks passed, and the boy was still off to the side. He sat there quietly in his autistic world, seemingly wholly separate and apart from the class. Then one day, another child was sick, absent from school. The autistic boy stepped forward and said, "I want to dance her part." He knew the part cold! He knew every other part, too! The entire time while he was sitting there, seemingly separate and apart, dance had made a connection with him.

---

* Dancing to Defy Expectations Parade magazine March 21, 2010
http://www.parade.com/news/our-towns/2010/0321-dubuque-iowa-dancing-to-defy-expectations.html

Dance opened up his world. And through dance, he was able to communicate.

I think about the autistic boy who was able to dance and I have high hopes that my son will one day find his own way to rise higher.

It is autumn. Golden leaves are falling, framing the double-pane window. I walk into PNB's studio to take a class with the great Bulgarian dancer Stanko Milov. He is well over six feet tall and towers over me, a great Herculean sculpted mass of muscle and form, as I demurely say good morning. The *Barré* is terrific. I have a great class. He is very funny and charismatic. He urges us to look out the window to see the tree full of glowing red leaves, and asks us to admire the tree as if he were giving an astute instruction about foot placement when coming out of *glissade*. I think about my husband, *my dearest Joseph,* and how lucky I am to have a man whom I love and who really cares about me. We are two halves of the same soul. A gust of wind sweeps up the golden leaves and they swirl in a chaotic dance of gold, red and light.

When I feel sad and do not know why, I acknowledge that I am feeling a bit lost and then I take a dance class. That is all that I need to do to remember. I feel nostalgia for New York. I remember my father and I miss him. I remember my grandmother Katherine. I miss her. I miss her tenement. I miss her steps. I have a powerful epiphany about what life is really about—reaching and extending one's self. Steps.

After I had been training in dance for several years, it dawned on me. We do not dance with any sort of tradition, custom or degree of regularity as part of our cultural experience. We are fine as spectators, watching amazing professionals dance. But why don't we ourselves dance?

One night before Christmas, I was walking through the *Seattle Center* and I passed through the *Center House,* which has an international food court and a miniature toy train and village on display. There is a small stage that from time-to-time features artistic cultural performances. I had unwittingly stumbled upon Latvian and Estonian folk dancing; a group of senior women were wearing colorful swirling skirts and knee britches with garters. They danced in pairs, facing forward, locked arm-in-arm, then taking two steps, a shuffling gait forward, and a grand stomping of their feet twice in unison. There was a lyrical rocking to and fro, a few light turns, and then the pattern repeated itself.

The women were serious and joyful and communing among themselves in a way that exemplified the full expression of "being together." Their dance was not at all about athletic or artistic prowess; it was a pure and powerful demonstration of how much they cared about being with one another. They, too, were rising higher.

In ballet class, I often practice rising higher by standing on one leg. I pull one leg high into *passé*, and tuck it in crosswise against my standing leg as if I am a pelican. On my standing leg, I rise high in *relevé* onto the ball of my foot, achieving the posture of a perfect tiptoe. Straight back, lifted torso, rising tall, eyes up, I let go of the *Barré* and stand solidly on one leg. The purpose of this training is preparation to do turns. My fascination with standing on one leg makes me wonder what it would be like not to have a leg. The practice of standing on one leg makes me wonder what it would take to rise higher, even if I only have one leg on which to stand.

You may have seen Anthony Robles in the news. He's not a dancer, but a champion wrestler who moves with the passion and grace of the most ardent *balletomane*. His bright yellow wrestling singlet shines, richly complementing his warm brown skin. Anthony is the young man from Arizona State University who recently won the 125-pound wrestling title at the 2011 NCAA Division 1 Wrestling Championships. What is notable about Anthony Robles—aside from the fact that he is young, handsome and Hispanic—is his missing leg. Anthony Robles was born without a right leg. Not having a leg puts a whole different spin on being a champion wrestler!

The essence of Anthony Robles is about how he honed and perfected his strengths and minimized his weaknesses. Robles told an Associated Press reporter, "My parents raised me to believe I could do whatever I set my mind to. I grew up thinking that way. I didn't think of my condition as something that could hold me back. I just thought, this is how God made me and I'm going to make the best of it."

According to several reports, when Robles was a toddler, he was fitted with a prosthetic leg. At age three, he tore off the leg and refused to wear it again.

Robles told the Associated Press, "Don't stay concerned with the negatives—what can hold me back, what my disadvantages are. I stay focused on the positive things—what I have, what I can do."

When asked about the challenges he faced as a wrestler, Robles said, "It doesn't have to be a missing leg; you could have any obstacle in your life. Whatever that is, you don't have to let it prevent you from doing things. You don't have to let the negativity of people or the doubters stop you from going after your dreams."*

According to some sports observers, as a sophomore and junior, Robles tended at critical moments to forget the mantra "play your game." He did not lead with his own strengths, resulting in losses in the NCAA tournament. But as a senior,

---

* What obstacle? Arizona State wrestler brings career to perfect end
By BOB BAUM / The Associated Press | Posted: Friday, March 25, 2011
http://huskerextra.com/mobile/article_1c4ab06b-3803-5025-a7ff-58ba1de4cc13.html

he consistently transformed his physical disadvantage into a competitive advantage.

Robles made his opponent play to his own great strength, which was his massively powerful upper torso. He had developed his upper body to become a formidable force to leverage—Robles is famous for his ability to swiftly lift and tilt his opponent's body in a single powerful sweep. Robles' disability became the source of his great strength. His upper body was larger than his opponents' upper bodies because his weight did not include a second leg.

Anthony Robles put his school, Arizona State University, on the proverbial wrestling map. On March 19, 2011, before a crowd of 18,000 in Philadelphia at the NCAA Division 1 Wrestling Championships, the 5'8", 125-pound Robles overpowered defending NCAA champion Matt McDonough by a score of 7-1. In fact, Robles' entire senior year at Arizona State had hit the mark of wrestling perfection—a 36-0 record.

Anthony Robles' missing leg may be a moot point. With or without a disability, Anthony Robles is a champion for all time, and serves as a lesson for us all. Robles maximized his strength and minimized his weaknesses. He developed a strategic game plan and stuck to it. We all deal with our own frailties and weaknesses, but there is something to be gained by having a profound sense of knowing who you are. When you lead with your strengths, people rarely see your weaknesses. When you stand tall on one leg, no one notices that your other leg is missing.

It does not matter what discipline you choose to learn to move well. I prefer ballet, because if you can gain some proficiency, you can learn to dance in any form or style. In the beginning, training as an adult might make you feel self-conscious, a bit foolish, and lacking in confidence. Do you want to stumble all over yourself while the entire class is watching you? After I stumbled too many times to count, I have come to know that I don't care, the way I once did. The very process of stumbling became magical, made me certain of who I was as a person; it allowed me to rise higher.

Confidence is knowing who you are, what you have done, and what you can do. It also means you develop an intuition about what you might be able to do. Knowing what you might be able to do is an aspiration, something you are striving for; it is an ideal. Myths abound about confidence. If you look at the array of self-help products, books, videos, CDs and podcasts, the overriding message is that you should be confident, if not all the time, then most of the time. Confidence is integral to the American dream and the foundation of the Horatio Alger story of success. Any short supply of self-confidence is often viewed as failure.

The reality, though, is quite different. You may lack confidence, but that is not a terrible thing. You *should* doubt. You *should* worry. You *should* express some measure of trepidation and concern every time you begin a new venture, project or activity. Ironically, if you do not experience some concern, you will not do a very good job.

You are bombarded by confidence programs and webinars that promise that, if your ratio of positive to negative thoughts is less than 3:1, you will take years off of your life, and that your doubting, questioning and self-critical thoughts will cause sickness, disease, all sort of unimaginable health problems and possibly an untimely death. Don't miss out on an opportunity to build confidence, the *confidence gurus* will tell you! Take this course, read this book, listen to this CD and in 30 days, you will gain a huge boost in your self-esteem. You hear about how confident people earn a much higher income over the course of their lifetimes. You hear how confident people make better first impressions, and have better relationships, better jobs, better sex, smarter children and larger homes. It's all about getting quick, easy, instant self-confidence at a discounted price.

None of these gurus or purveyors of confidence are wrong; they do have a relevant message, and some are even gifted psychologists. But they will encourage you to learn the facts about achieving confidence without embracing the *épaulement of knowing your own soul*. In ballet, the positioning of the shoulders, called *épaulement*, gives a sculpted, three-dimensional quality to the dancer's positions. It takes many years to develop this technique, in the same way that it takes time, training and discipline to develop genuine self-confidence rooted in the core of your being, coming from the essence of your soul.

You need to figure out which of these myths about confidence is fact and which is fiction, and what is the best way for you to achieve a bona fide physical, mental and spiritual confidence that prepares you to explore excellence.

At any age, ballet training is a confidence-builder. If you can dance less than perfectly in a room full of incredibly gifted professional dancers, then you can get over anything and always perform to the best of your ability. Lasting confidence comes from the willingness to do one more *Rond de Jambé* (going around the circle again) to develop the surety of knowing who who you are. Lasting confidence is about self-management. You take your anxiety or your worry and harness the energy to perform at a higher level. At the core of your brand, you will always find self-confidence, which develops from day-in, day-out practice, training, hard work and focus.

The more I trained in ballet, the more I wanted to squeeze ballet classes into my busy work schedule.

After a few months, I was taking classes on Monday and Wednesday nights. I worked miserably hard, vowing to go on toe (*en pointe*) within six months. But when the time came, I realized that my body was not ready to meet the appointed deadline. Most people go *en pointe* too early, and my desire was not unusual. One of the hardest choices to make is to know when you are ready to rise higher and when you are not. Without enough training, your body doesn't have the form, muscularity or strength to achieve alignment and balance on toe shoes. The same principle applies when you are building a business or building a brand. Unless you have the experience, credentials, and training, you don't have the skill set necessary to build a brand that will achieve alignment with your business.

How do you know when to rise higher? Throughout the years of building my PR business, I have known many people who wanted overnight success. They believed that just by hiring me, they would achieve instant fame and recognition. These were always the most difficult clients, because they had expectations that were wildly out of alignment with their experience and sometimes with their talent, expertise, even their business models. Too many people do not understand that the discipline needed to develop a solid reputation is the same in intensity as the training a ballet dancer must undergo to become technically proficient. Too many people do not know how to place their feet in first position, and yet they want to be able to do triple turns and amazing jumps. Or they think a few classes will automatically make them land in the right position.

After stumbling upon Annie de Vuono's class at Belltown Ballet five years ago, I knew I did not know how to place my feet in first position. From a purely spiritual standpoint, taking my first classes were the same as when I was a child and climbed steps in an old brown tenement in Yonkers. Now, many classes later, I look at my feet in fifth position and cannot help but note that my turnout has improved.

After five years, or 1,500 hours of training, I felt like I was doing more than training in ballet. I felt like I was starting to dance! I started seeing little signs that I might be learning to develop *épaulement*, which is much more than the way I hold my head or my shoulders. I was starting to feel a natural grace that was more powerful than anything I have ever known.

It has taken over five years to get to this space and time, to a place where I am who I should be and am confident with knowing my own destiny. When you think about it, a ballerina has a lot in common with a Benedictine monk. Both keep going around the same circle, a *Rond de Jambé*, to get to a higher place. Soaring—It took much more time, discipline, commitment, sheer will, focus, and outright defiance than one can learn in a weekend retreat with a spiritual guide who does not know how to dance. *I am soaring beyond where I ever thought I could go!*

Twyla Tharp once said, "I have the wherewithal to challenge myself for my entire life. That's a great gift." At PNB, I remember Alexandra Dickson saying "Up, up, up." That's what it's all about, moving ever upward.

The desire to rise higher is a great gift. How do you know when to rise higher? In some ways, the answer is purely intuitive. You just know when the time has come. Dance is the physical articulation of a song that does not stop singing. I remember one of my favorite ballet teachers, a Russian woman who teaches at PNB. *Tatiana* is a woman of a certain age with intense green eyes. Her turnout is 180 degrees and the arch and point of her feet is ballet perfection. She left her career in dance early, but she is a gifted teacher. She has a way of teaching musicality in movement that is exceptional. She often said, "When you are moving, you listen to the music, and the music does not just end, but the final note lingers and continues to resound for a time." As it should also be with your body and your dancing, you will linger on the final phrase, as if you are going to continue to move. So how do you rise higher? You wait until you hear the song that does not stop singing. Then you have no choice but to rise higher.

There are times when ballet forces you to travel in the same orbit as the sun and the moon. When my daughters were little, they used to say they were heavenly bodies: Katie was the sun and Sarah was the moon. Each one had her own orbit, and the sun and the moon became metaphors for their lives. Katie, goddess of the sun, has an astute business mind and works as a manager for Nordstrom's. Sarah of many moons has her heart set on becoming an astronaut and shares my love of dance. I was thinking of Katie and Sarah when I was in ballet class one week at PNB.

Oleg Gorboulev was the instructor. I have to confess that I have an affinity for Russian instructors. Since I started training, I have had four Russian teachers. I find there is something about their *Barré* and the way they make you move on the floor that pushes me out of my comfort zone and on to a higher level. In disciplines other than dance, the Russians have developed expert techniques for training older athletes who are well past their prime—helping them to achieve a higher level of performance.

Oleg made us do a *sauté* + rapid waltz turn+ *sauté de Basque* in our own circle, and in an outer circle traveling the perimeter around the room. I was terrified, because I am not used to traveling in my own orbit. I was in a larger circle spinning around the perimeter of the room alone, except for the other equally terrified dancer, who was moving in her own circle from the opposite corner of the room. I traveled like the moon in its own orbit, going around the earth and going around the sun. I was dizzy, battling vertigo and was afraid of falling, but I never came close to feeling like I actually would fall. I only know that this movement was terrifying and challenging enough to make me want to do it again. I want my daughters to know that we can often do what at first seems to be as impossible, even if it is reaching for the sky to move like the sun and the moon.

When the time comes to rise higher, you will know, when three signs appear. First, you are riddled by self-doubt, with a touch of despair and humility. You are not sure you can rise to the next level. *Your best work should always spring from healthy self-doubt.* We all come to ballet and to life with this equal measure of humility and courage. First, to do something well, you must experience doubt. Supreme self-confidence or over confidence makes bad ballet dancers and bad businesspeople. Second, you must be firmly committed to the hard work and dedication that will take you to the next level. You will do whatever it takes. Third, you really do not want to undertake the challenge. You are comfortable where you are and you do not want to suffer. Rising higher inevitably always causes some pain, but brings an ample measure of reward. You hear the voice prodding you upward. This is the same voice I heard that first commanded me to dance. You hear the voice. You try to ignore it. You are Jesus in the Garden of Gethsemane, and you do not want to drink from the cup. You do not want to be crucified. But you are the son of God and you have no choice.

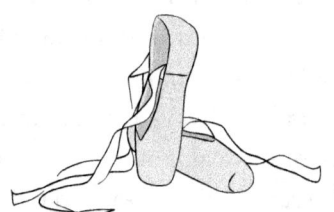

— 6 —

Balance

When I was four, I lived in my grandmother's tenement for four months while my mother was in the hospital. My father worked many hours and was unable to care for a small child. I wonder what my life would have been like if I had gone to live with my father's relatives in the Italian neighborhood. When my father came to see me, he told me soon I would go home. It's not that I did not believe him. But I was a child who had lost my mother; I didn't believe anyone. Even then, I knew my life had changed forever. The Steps became my new home. The Steps became a place I could always go to learn about my strength or come to terms with a part of me that, until then, had remained undiscovered.

One time I went back to New York shortly after I left law school. I found myself staying with my grandmother Katherine in the old brown tenement on Jackson Street. The steps inside the tenement were still the same, only then, as a 25-year-old woman, I could see the ancient turquoise surface was made from old-fashioned textured linoleum. The size and shape of the steps were uneven and jagged. The steps made for the working class and poor immigrants were rough-hewn and formed in many shapes and sizes. Imperfect or not, these steps were still a source of comfort to me and the place inside of me that I still call home.

My grandmother lived alone on the first floor of the tenement. Her husband, my grandfather, Dick Sheedy, had been dead for many years. His overstuffed recliner still held the prominent spot in the front of the living room. His old metal ashtray sat on a side table and held a lone wooden pipe, as if she expected him to come home soon and fill it to the brim with tobacco. I remember a mirror, three panels framing thick glass, hanging high in the middle of the wall above the couch. A small black-and-white television sat at the other end of the room, where it was perfectly positioned for my grandfather to watch it from his overstuffed chair. A narrow coffee table was decorated with lace doilies and a bowl full of nuts, whole in their shells, waiting to be cracked open with a silver nutcracker.

Her bathtub always had about an inch of gray, standing water—a habit she had formed during the Great Depression, when nothing was wasted, not even bathwater, which she used each night to wash her stockings.

I remember wearing all black: a black sweater, a black velvet skirt, black pumps, and pearls. I was going into the city for dinner with my childhood best friend at Tavern on the Green in Central Park. Before I left for dinner, grandmother and I sat in the kitchen, which still had relics from another era: a big metal dry sink made of white-enameled metal drawers, pull-out trays and cabinets. Long before kitchens had the luxury of built-in cabinets, the poor and working class had dry sink cabinets. The tiny gas stove and oven had to be ignited with a match. Grandmother's pots were made from the old heavy-gauge aluminum; most of them didn't have matching covers. She had a single flat metal lid, a one-size-fits-all top that covered every pot.

From the dry sink cabinet, my grandmother pulled out a box that held faded picture albums, the kind that used small pasted paper acorns to fasten the photos to pages of black parchment paper. For hours, we thumbed through the photos. She showed me pictures of so many people, relatives long dead, whose names I still don't know. That night was about as close as I would ever get to my grandmother.

If only she knew that many years later, I would take up dance and remember her home and its steps. Maybe in some odd way, she did know. Old people are funny that way; they just know things. It was the last time I was there, at the old brown tenement on 67 Jackson Street. I will never forget that place.

Whenever I take the "open" classes at PNB with Bruce Wells, he uses his lyrical phrase "The river runs back," to give instructions when you are moving forward on the floor so you know that in the next movement, you will be turning back. "The river runs back" is a beautiful and powerful way to describe how you are about to change the course of your direction. Doing so always requires a superb mastery of balance. "The river runs back" is also another way to revisit your past—again—and to see it in a new and different way.

At PNB, Julie Tobiason always asked her students, "Where is your balance point?" And here I am, years later, trying to learn if my balance point is always in the same place. Some days I am more certain of my balance than on other days.

For many hours, I have thought about the concept of balance. I think achieving balance is easy to talk about, but harder to do. Balance is a precarious state. Losing one's balance means you can fall. Balance is about the scales perpetually in a state of motion: rising up and moving down. It is rare when scales are perfectly balanced.

More often than not, you are the one seeking balance. Balance does not go looking for you, knock on your door and say, "Stand there with one leg on the ground, and raise the other leg high and straight into the air." There is much more to maintaining equilibrium than appearing to be calm, accepting and tolerant. While trying to achieve balance in ballet, I have found I could do one thing exceptionally well and another thing very poorly, only moments apart. I feel the same way about this process of the yin and yang, the duality of our ability to perform well or not, as I do about the ability to attain balance in both ballet and in business.

One of the most beautiful movements in ballet is called *The Promenade*. In a classical ballet production, you will see a ballerina hold her leg up in *arabesque* as the male dancer strolls around her, holding her gently by the hand and turning her around 360 degrees as she stands on one leg *en pointe*. The male dancer holds her hand as if to lend support, but it is the ballerina who is sustaining the balance.

When you learn *The Promenade*, there is no male to support you as you pivot around in a full revolution while standing on one leg. You simply hold your leg up in a lovely position in full *arabesque* or complete *attitude*, while you turn around on your standing leg in a full circle, 360 degrees. This is not as easy as it sounds. It can be a critical test of your balance and control. If you can do a full *Promenade* without wobbling or allowing the leg you have lifted into the air to drop lower or fall, that is a significant achievement.

Every ballet class at an intermediate level or above requires you to practice *The Promenade*. Ballet class is as structured and ritualistic as performing the liturgy in the Catholic Church. The rituals and movements are progressive, from the simplest *tendu* at the *Barré* to performing complicated *fouette* turns. The class begins easily enough, focusing on the basics, and becomes progressively more challenging, adding steps and sequences to new combinations you have barely had time to learn or master.

First, you always warm up at the *Barré*. The *Barré* is a loose term applied to any horizontal handrail constructed out of metal or wood. Some are standing and moveable, and others are built into the wall. The exercises practiced at the *Barré* are designed to warm up and strengthen an assortment of small muscles that are only made identifiable in a well-trained ballet body. The *Barré* is preparation for the more challenging combinations that are performed on the floor. There is a natural progression from the slow *adagio* to the more rapid *petite* and *grande allegros,* which incorporate faster footwork and multiple types of turns and jumps.

A good *Barré* truly prepares you for the rigors of floor work and warms your muscles enough to reduce the risk of injury. A well taught *Barré* sequence introduces a succession of exercises that grow progressively more challenging by testing your flexibility and increasing your strength so that are ready to dance. One teacher, Stephanie Cain, always said there was nothing natural about ballet. In fact, every position should feel awkward. Over time, though, the more you train, the more some of the most unnatural posturing in ballet suddenly comes to feel as if it is normal. You will want to fully extend your leg, contract your muscles, and point your toe.

Every time I practice *The Promenade*, I begin my journey not knowing if I will make the full circle without dropping or lowering the leg that I am holding high in the air. Some days my balance is better than other days. Some days my balance is completely off, and I stumble around and cannot explain why. Strong balance requires discipline, training and focus, and while you are in the midst of balancing, you have to actually relax into it, and achieve sort of a Zen-like state. Balance is precarious.

From one day to the next, I cannot predict how well I will hold and maintain my balance. It is unaffected by lack of sleep, poor diet, stress or illness. There are days when I have arrived at class in New York City after being on a plane all night, and my balance was strong. Then one time, after I rode a train for four hours from Boston to New York City, arrived in Penn Central in the middle of a rainstorm and dragged my bags to Broadway, hailed a cab amid a crowd rushing out from Madison Square Garden, and landed in class on the Upper West Side on time, my balance was shaky. Once I had a glass of champagne at my daughter's bridal shower and then afterward went to a class; my balance was stellar. I only know one thing for certain: The more I practice, the better I am able to achieve balance.

One of the most central components of balance is related to economy, both the *economy of movement* and the economic realities of business. During my fourth year of ballet training, I was in a class at PNB with Elaine Bauer. She spoke about achieving an economy of movement—of keeping each step small and precise enough to seamlessly move and blend into the next step. When you first learn to dance, each step you take tends to be too large, overdone and uncoordinated, so the movement from step-to-step is unstable, shaky; there tends to be a whole lot of jerking around. It wasn't until my fifth year of training that Annie de Vuono commented one day that I was achieving economy of movement. "Don't you feel it?" she asked.

Economy of movement has greater ramifications than controlling the precision and range of your steps. In my fifth year of training, in another class with Elaine Bauer, she spoke about using your mind to think ahead or to plan for your next move, even if that next move is 6, 7, and 8… down the road in the sequence. It is amazing and powerful to think about moving your body strategically. You might be actively engaged in the moment and doing one step now, but at the same time you must focus on the steps yet to come so that the entire movement is connecting with greater economy, precision, and above all else, fluidity.

In business, you are often engaged in an action or a battle, but it is not the single action you are engaged in that is important. It is the fifth, eighth or tenth action down the road that can harm you or cause damage to your business. It is the action down the road that we must prepare for while we are operating in the present. What we do now has major ramifications on what will happen in the future.

My practice of ballet represents the strategic movement between the two worlds—a balancing act from ballet class back to the business office. I start my work day between 5 a.m. and 6 a.m. Mid-morning, I take "lunch," which is usually a ballet class or Pilates. Sometimes I take a long brisk walk or I go to the gym to cycle and lift weights. My work schedule is brutal, but I will not miss my workouts. I am doing much more than practicing ballet. I am committed to exploring excellence.

How long will it take to achieve mastery? Later in the same day after I had taken a class with Elaine Bauer, I was thinking about practicing *economy of movement*. I also happened to be doing Business Intelligence research for a client. I saw an interview with author and pundit Malcolm Gladwell, who said it takes at least 10,000 hours to become an expert. *For you to master anything will take far longer than you think it will take.* In the last five years, I have logged in about 1,500 hours practicing ballet. In terms of mastery, I have a long way to go, and I don't know if I will get there. My greatest satisfaction is derived from the journey. In my pursuit of excellence, I am exploring my body, mind, heart and soul. I am who I am now, and I am on the road to becoming who I am destined to be.

Any decision you make requires an assessment of its economy and balance. You have to weigh what's good for you, in balance with what is good for someone else. This is a fundamental utilitarian principle at the root of the economic theory conceived by the mathematician John Nash (for which he won the Nobel Prize). If you find yourself making decisions that are only good for you, then your decisions are selfish and are not helpful to anyone else. If you are only making decisions that are good for others, then you are harming yourself by being too self-less. You are engaging in martyr-like behavior. This principle can get complex. You must assess the finer points of every situation so you can make a good decision that will govern your steps both here and now, and in the future. The best decisions are the ones you make by strategically balancing between two worlds: you, and everything else.

In your strategic movement between two worlds, balance becomes an economic argument. Balance is what you weigh in every situation governing life or business. You ask yourself: what is good for you and the group? You will go back and forth. You are assessing the situation and weighing the possibilities. Some decisions will be weighted in your favor; other decisions will lean toward favoring the group. You can never weigh too heavily toward you or too heavily toward the group. To lean one way or the other risks becoming unbalanced. There always has to be give-and-take between you and the group.

Who is the group? The group is your company, your job, your co-workers, your clients, your vendors, your family, your children, your spouse, your friends, your club, your church or your temple. Who keeps score? You are the scorekeeper. You are the keeper of the balance.

You need to take one small step. You need to assess your current situation completely, accurately, and fairly. You must describe your situation without interjecting your own opinion. You must give a simple narration of the facts. Your assessment is a complete movement in balance.

In business, when you are assessing balance, look at the numbers. Numbers usually tell the truth. At the end of the year, study where you spent money. What was your return on investment? It's simple math.

Every year I undertake pro-bono work for good causes or for non-profits. I carefully choose my pro-bono clients and find, more often than not, that their core mission resonates with my own passionate beliefs about what makes the world a better place. And while I do not ever expect financial remuneration for pro-bono work, I do regard it as a rainmaker to draw paid work, and I give it a year to materialize. When you are working for people—without getting payment—there is a certain implicit understanding that they must refer business to you by recommending you and your work. This is the nature of business. It is a matter of balance. It is an economic argument. If what is good for the group is not ever going to be good for you, then you need to rethink your commitment.

The same principle applies to love, friendship and family, but it is a trickier equation of balance. In assessing the give-and-take of human relationships, it is not so easy. Emotions cloud our judgment, and there is no simple factoring of how much is spent, relative to how much you receive in return. As a woman, a friend, a mother, a daughter, a lover, and a wife, some days the scales of balance tilt wildly in one direction or the other. It is an emotionally feasible question: Are you the one giving, more often than not? Are you the one turning in *The Promenade*? Or are you the one extending your hand to offer support so you can be the ballast? In the *Promenade of life*, you must have your chance to be the prima ballerina and have all attention focused on you. So when that time comes for me to fly into your arms, can you do a lift?

There is a single exclusion to the dual principle of economy and balance. Sometimes you need to give a gift. A gift has no strings attached. A gift has no expectations. Your gift is the willingness to extend yourself in some way for the sole purpose of enriching another human being. Your gift may be expanding another person's potential for growth. The gift is many things:

it is a compliment, a gesture, a smile, or a tangible thing, like money, goods and services. A gift is an extension of your heart. In ballet, when a teacher corrects me, she has given me a gift that will allow me to become a better dancer.

It is funny when you consider during the life and times of my grandmother Katherine, people did not talk about business and branding; instead, they talked about reputation. They talked about how one rotten bastard could spoil a whole bushel of apples. People built reputations, in large part, by whom they associated with, who their family was, and where they lived. It had little to do with defining your core brand attributes and implementing a PR outreach program that got the word out about you and your brand. If you grew up in Yonkers on the wrong side of Nepperhan Avenue, you didn't get a chance to be a good apple.

In our new mobile society, no one cares where you came from; people only care about what you can do for them, and how well you can *dance, metaphorically speaking.* How well you can dance has more to do with your positioning and your performance—the literal act of dancing, which is really about how well you are perceived by your audience.

Building one's reputation is suddenly all about perception. How well do you balance between your perception of yourself and the perception of how your audience sees you?

Building your reputation means you must balance the three legs of the stool. You need to identify the right press who would be interested in telling your story—the story of you, and how what you do changes the world in some small way that is newsworthy enough to become news. You need to use the right blend of social media to build your community, online and in real life. You need to spend time to nurture these genuine relationships with people who care about who you are and what you do. These three legs—press, social media and networking—are as simple as a *Rond de Jambé*, going around the circle, one more time. You keep going around the circle to learn about your life and to live your destiny.

Delivering a perfect pitch to the media is a lot like achieving balance. A person who is blind achieves balance by training all his other senses to become more acute and so, in a sense, his balance is more sensitive and more perfect than a person who can see. Sight-impaired or not, balance requires all of your senses to be working in unison. It is important for me to be "in balance" and to work hard to achieve it.

When you pitch the media, a colleague or client, all of your senses have to work in unison, simultaneously, to achieve balance. While you are pitching, try closing your eyes and you will flail around. I found if I was standing on one leg and if I shut my eyes, I would wobble and have to catch myself so I would not fall. This is a great metaphor for pitching. If you close your eyes, you will stumble, you could fall and you will not deliver a perfect pitch. How do you know if your pitch is perfect? You can feel it, as surely as you can stand securely on one leg.

There are moves in ballet that seem to be nothing more than an articulation of balance, but they are actually much more complex. At a Saturday class at PNB, Michele Golden Curtis asked us to *Develope* to the front, then to the back in *Arabesque*, then a small quarter-turn to center and then *Develope* to the side. Easy enough, isn't it? Michele described this movement as "simple, but very challenging." So the challenge comes with each *Develope*. You do not know how far you will be able to extend your leg perfectly taut and straight, all the way out to your pointed toe. And each time you shift from leg to leg, there is the full understanding that it is the standing leg that is doing all the work, even though the working leg is extending as far as it possibly can, striking out into the air like a lightning rod. And through all of this, you must be composed and truly relaxed, because if you are tense, inevitably you will wobble, stumble, lose your extension, and could even fall.

Most of the time, you will not fall. It is much more likely that you will drop your leg and start all over again, the same way I return to the old tenement steps of my heart. Climbing steps: you would think that should be easy to do; the movement should be rote by now. You would think I would know the way. If I did, I would not keep returning to this same place. I'd let the steps from my childhood at the old brown tenement go away. But in my mind, I return to visit the old tenement that had a front stoop and a back stoop. I see the interior walls, made thick with twelve layers of wallpaper and shellac. I see the small, dark lobby, with its stone floor and a heavy inner-sanctum-type door that kept the warm air locked in and the cold air out. The reason why I keep returning to these steps is because no matter how many times I climb them, they remain simple, but challenging. I am no longer a child, but somewhere deep inside, I am young and willing to learn.

When I was thirteen, I wanted to dance. But throughout my childhood, my mother was sick and required frequent care. Somehow my father found a dance studio in Bronxville. I took three buses to get there. My teacher's name was Florence Castanza, and her claim to fame was her brief career as a dancer at the London Palladium. With her thick brown wiry hair and tough, leathery skin, Florence appeared to be old. She didn't exude the grace of a dancer, but she was small, quick on her feet and energetic. She spent most of the class teaching us *petite allegro* combinations, little jumps in *Coupé*, and seemed intent on training us to become a corps of Irish Step Dancers. The classes were small and even though I wanted to dance, I had no way of knowing that this class would not give me the serious dance training that I needed.

I was very flexible, so much so that I had "trick knees." While

I was walking, my knee would sometimes suddenly dislocate. It was often painful. Most of the time, my knee would just rotate back into place on its own. Then one day, I was playing kickball out on the street and I slid on the road, which was slick with car oil. I landed twisted, in a completely lateral position, which not only dislocated my knee but seemed to tear something. I could not walk. I never knew what sort of injury had occurred. Arthroscopic surgery was not available. The doctor said I needed to be on crutches for six weeks. Not that it matters now. I only know that it broke my rhythm, taking the long bus trips to the dance studio in Bronxville and studying with Florence Castanza, whom I never saw again.

I didn't encounter ballet again for several years, until I moved to a new high school and found Carmen Canavan. I used to accompany her to a dance class somewhere in Columbus Circle—a little hole in the wall—with a small hardwood floor in dire need of refinishing. The dance instructor was a middle-aged Russian man, small, a bit portly, thick in the middle, but he had a warm smile and intelligent eyes. Carmen sprang across the floor, doing *grand jetes* like she was a young fawn.

For the longest time after high school, I did not know what had happened to Carmen. I did hear that she won a scholarship to the Joffrey Ballet. We fell out of touch.

Martha Graham said, "Some men have thousands of reasons why they cannot do what they want to, when all they need is one reason why they can." I took up ballet during a time in my life when I was looking for some deep spiritual meaning that I knew I could not find in a church. I have had many experiences with faith and religion, some good, some not so good, and some awful. I am confused by the demands made by religion and, more often than not, I find that religion is a terrible beauty. I am close to Jews (some Orthodox Jews), Christians (some Evangelical), good Catholics and Episcopalians, and a core contingency of

Hindus, Buddhists, Sufis and Sikhs, atheists, agnostics, and new-ageists. I see all religion as simply an attempt by human beings to understand an irrational and contradictory world. We create God in our own image by making Him a simple-minded traffic cop who enforces the rules that we have already made up for Him.

I wanted to connect with something larger than myself, yet I wasn't seeking community. I was seeking a connection, a way for me to explore and reach part of a larger whole. In my ideal world, balance means that each person is another face of God. With dance, you only have you and your own body to work with; you must play your body, as if it was a magnificent cello. Dance reaches the highest ideal of human potential. Dance is the closest art to God, or the art that achieves a pure state of perfection most like God. Dance is what, I hope, God must see.

Choreographer George Balanchine said, "God creates, I do not create. I assemble and I steal everywhere to do it—from what I see, from what the dancers can do, from what others do."

Whether you believe in God or not does not matter. Ballet is full of stops and starts, small, incremental improvements, half-measures, half-hearted attempts and dismal failures. But there is always a brief glimmer in time when some part of your movement is working beautifully. For me, ballet is my working metaphor for defying gravity and reaching for the sky, all the while maintaining my balance.

If balance is at the heart of ballet, then you can see how dangerous it is to take risks in business and still maintain balance. There is a risk inherent in doing any intense activity in order to achieve your business goals. It is not within our cultural norms or expectations to make a practice out of repeated failure. The thought of failure makes us ashamed and not want to try. We become petrified, isolated and stand frozen in time. And yet, through my years of adult ballet training, I have learned that in my many attempts to dance well, it is my repeated failure that has eventually liberated my body, mind and soul. It's like James Brown said: "Any problem in the world can be solved by dancing."

In business, every time I make a mistake, I have unknowingly trained myself to keep going, to keep driving forward as if I have never missed a beat.

But even after five years of ballet training, the *grand jeté* eluded me. One Tuesday, I took a particularly difficult class—it was an open intermediate class with Bruce Wells—that was full of PNB corps dancers and only a few dilettantes. Even many of the most practiced dilettantes had trained extensively as children. Some of them were practically children in age. And then, there was me.

I did it to myself again. I took a risk and failed, I thought, walking briskly from ballet class across Mercer Street and preparing myself for the climb up the steepest hill in Seattle. For a half a block, I berated myself for doing the *grand jeté* so poorly, and then I stopped. It was time to stop being critical. How many women my age are training in ballet? How many people who are training in ballet then immediately after class walk up the steepest hill in Seattle? I began to think about all the little moments when I did not-so-terrible ballet. My turns had improved. My *promenade* was gaining stability. My posture was terrific, and I was in awesome shape. I took the hill like a Roman warrior, the same way I climbed steps as a child. No one can stop me. I will dance as long as I can. And I will take my *attitude* with me everywhere I go. One day I may even be able to do a superb *grand jeté*.

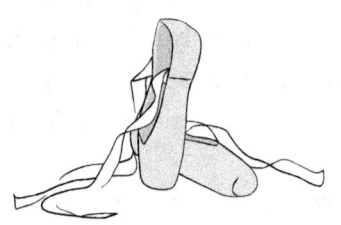

— 7 —
Fall and Recovery

Life is a collection of slow deaths and slower births. Each time I encounter the steps at my grandmother's house, I believe I will climb them. I believe I will make it to the top. I believe I will not fall or fail. I believe I will always find these steps as long as I am alive. But sooner or later, I will climb those steps for the last time.

There are days when I still remember what it was like to live there. My great-grandparents Mary and Simon Mulqueen once lived on the first floor, and my grandparents Katherine and Dick Sheedy lived upstairs in the second floor apartment, where they raised four children, one of whom was my mother. Simon had a notorious reputation as a binge drinker.

One day Simon was sitting on the back stoop during a thunderstorm drinking a boilermaker, a lethal combination of beer chased by whiskey. A lightning bolt hit close by and knocked the metal beer stein from his hand. He heard a voice commanding him never to drink again. Not everyone gets the *thunderbolt* treatment from God! It seems to be a phenomenon that is peculiar to this particular family. And Simon did stop drinking. Years later, after he died, I, being a naughty child, stole his cane and ran around the house, then tried to climb the steps with a limping gait and a heavy heart, the same way he did.

It's a funny feeling to want to live in a house that is no longer there. It's not like it's your old house that was sold long ago and just happens to be inhabited by people whom you do not know. The house is only an image in your own mind. No one has lived in this house the way you lived there. Only you know the secrets that you shared with the house. And now the house is gone forever. And when you pass on, all the secrets you have shared with the house will die, too.

If the place was mine, I would fix it up and live there again. Had I lived there before it burned to the ground, I would have fought to win back the old tenement. I have lived a lifetime of sticking up for myself and winning. I have battled some mighty tough contenders, and I have won. When the going gets rough, I return to the old brown tenement in my mind and climb its steps. It is where I fight all my battles and win.

My grandmother's image and likeness comes to mind like one of the blurry photographs she showed me during the last night we spent together in the old tenement. If I want to remember what she looked like, all I have to do is look into the mirror. Everyone said we looked identical, except my eyes are green and hers were blue. She was a brunette, and I am a blonde. Her middle name was *Patricia,* and I am her namesake. We are different people. Her daily rituals had a sameness that spilled over to all other aspects of her life. She rarely traveled, had never been on a plane, and stayed within an eight-block perimeter that spanned from Getty Square to St. Mary's Church, where she attended mass at noon most every day of her life. She prayed for everyone, lit candles for perpetual devotion, gave alms to the poor, and like everyone else on the Irish side of my family, she heard voices.

On a sunny September day, I did hear a voice commanding me to dance. God spoke: He said *Dance!* And I listened. I have had some practice listening to this voice. This was not the first time, and it will not be the last time. The voice can be quite bothersome. Although I know the commands are always in my best interest that does not mean I have to like them. Practicing ballet the way someone else would practice going to church means that every now and then, I have to take a hard fall, learn a lesson and make a recovery.

I am not afraid of falling. But I regard falling as being close to failure. I still ponder whether falling and failing are the same? Falling and the recovery from a fall is a symbol of the struggle between failure and triumph that you must engage in throughout your life. It is a fundamental tension. If you want to do anything exceptional in life, you must embrace the inevitable prospect of falling.

There is a great risk inherent in doing any physical activity as intense as ballet. Falling is a real possibility. In fact, falling is inevitable. Sooner or later, you will fall. When you fall in ballet, the image of falling is clear. You hit the ground and land in an unflattering pose. More often than not, when you do fall, you will land in a controlled setting. There is no softer landing than coming down on a sprung floor in a ballet studio. To not engage in a discipline that tests your balance will most certainly guarantee that you will fall. As we grow older, one of the first things we lose is our balance. Engaging in ballet, yoga, Pilates, some form of balance training minimizes the natural deterioration of your sense of balance.

One day I was in class, and one of the more advanced dancers simply fell off the *Barré* and landed in a heap on the floor. I can't tell you why she fell. I don't think she could explain why she fell. Sometimes falling is a mystery. It is something you need to do to from time to time; you need to experience getting up from the floor.

As always, ballet training invites physical danger—the same risk associated with doing any intense physical activity. During my days as an adult dancer, I have seen many falls and injuries.

During my classes, I noted one woman who was quite large, pushing about 180 pounds. She was a heavy dancer, and I don't mean solely her weight. Her movements were grand and when she came down from a jump, you could hear her smack the floor. I also noticed that despite her weight, she moved so beautifully on the floor. She had a lyrical quality that blended seamlessly with the music and her movement. She had an archival memory that I did not have for putting together the steps in a sequence. Then one Saturday, we were doing *glissades* into *pas de chats* and she came down hard, so hard there was the sound of a staccato pop like a firecracker. She came to a stop. She could not step on her foot. She tried putting her foot down gingerly, repeatedly, but her foot was injured. Holding her injured leg *en passé* like an injured bird, she hobbled on one leg out of the studio. It happened three years ago. I never saw her again.

No one else had stopped dancing. Dancers do not stop for the wounded. The teacher will not necessarily inquire what happened. You must walk off the floor alone, like a wounded soldier leaving the battlefield. No matter how much the dancer is hurting, some things are best kept to one's self. The less said the better. A certain stoicism prevails. Sound heartless? The dance world can be as cold and as cruel a place as the business world. In business, if you get sick or lose a family member or incur some other mishap, the email does not stop flowing. Business does not stop. No one really cares about your mishap. Oh, people will offer condolences, but if your output should slow down for *too long*, you can expect that your business will decline and suffer.

If you must inevitably fall, then falling on the training ground of a sprung floor is preferable to the falls you take every day in life and in business. Through the years, I have come to determine that people fall for three reasons:

First, you experience unwanted trials and tribulations in life. Bad luck. One woman I know is married to a man who has multiple chronic illnesses and requires round-the-clock medical care. Another woman was returning to her car in a dark, unfamiliar garage. She lost her way, walked onto what she thought was a loading dock, and fell ten feet onto a concrete platform. She broke her back in multiple locations, and it was a full year before she could walk again. Sick child, accidents, lost jobs, unfair work situations, bad breaks: these are the things you cannot do anything about.

The second reason why you fall is because you didn't work hard enough, long enough or smart enough. You didn't do the hard work that it took to build your business. You didn't get into the ballet studio and train, whether you felt like it or not. You did not put the time in to do your best possible work. I have seen enormously untalented people succeed at their chosen craft—in art and in business—because they put in the time to achieve success. Their real talent was rooted in brilliant self-promotion and knowing how to connect with the right people who helped them to succeed.

The third reason is that falling may mean what you have set out to accomplish is not your true destiny. You are not being true to who you really are. You cannot run from who you really are. There is no way out. You must embrace everything destiny offers to you. If you are not true to your own identity, eventually you will take a mighty fall from grace from which there is no recovery.

Falling on a sprung floor trains you to learn how to gracefully pick yourself up off the ground, stand up tall, and continue dancing. Building your brand or your business should be as disciplined as going around the circle or doing a *Rond de Jambé* one more time. If you think it is hard, it is. You will learn to enjoy the difficulty and thrive on the great grace that is being given to you. If you think hard work is too difficult, then you need to ask yourself two questions: Do you have what it takes to succeed in your chosen profession? Is what you think you want to do really your destiny? If your answer to both of these questions is yes, then you must ask yourself a third question: Do you have what it takes to do the hard work to explore excellence?

One of the great pioneers of modern dance in the 20th century, Doris Humphrey, has developed a movement philosophy that embodies the principle of "Fall and Recovery." She defines it as "two conflicting, yet intertwining impulses, the desire to achieve perfection and stability, and the equally compelling urge to experience the danger of the 'wilder emotions,' the ecstasy of abandon." Tremendous freedom comes in any artistic movement, especially when you take the risk to dance as if you will never have this chance to dance again.

Darci Kistler, who danced with the New York City Ballet, is widely considered to be the last of George Balanchine's ballerinas. She came to his attention when she took an enormous fall in the main rehearsal hall. Balanchine reportedly loved when dancers fell—during rehearsal—because it meant that they were not playing it safe; they were taking a huge risk to reach for a higher level of excellence. After Balanchine's death, Darci Kistler went on to dance with the New York City Ballet for nearly thirty years.*

Despite Balanchine's delight at seeing his dancers fall when engaged in the pursuit of excellence, it is doubtful that he was fond of seeing his dancers fall during an actual performance. Training habitually and pushing for a greater demand of one's self in rehearsal, often seems to minimize the likelihood that you will fall when you are called upon to perform flawlessly.

---

* Darci Kistler Exits the Stage by TONI BENTLEY WSJ, May 28 2010
http://online.wsj.com/article/SB10001424052748704026204575266940794039822.html

We all fall, but it's the unanticipated falls that can take you out. The only redeeming aspect of a fall is the elegance with which you rise from the ground. Resilience is not something that can be taught by the wisest of instructors, even if they have the Rasputin-like intensity of someone as talented and as powerful as Balanchine. Falling is an art that is best expressed in how well you recover. What separates the great from the mediocre is the ability to fall and recover with some measure of grace.

At one dance studio where I go, there are groups of young dancers who are training to be in a company, waiting outside the door to come in after our adult class is finished. Sometimes they watch us, make faces, snicker, and on occasion, even laugh openly at us. I used to imagine that the young professional dancers who were watching me were thinking and wondering, why do I dance? Why did I put so much time into something that I would never be good at doing? I would never hit the lower rung of the ideal standard where they have already placed. I do not know how to explain to them that, even though I know I will never get as good as I want to be, that one small detail will not stop me from trying.

One time I was in an open ballet class. One of my favorite teachers just happened to be taking the same class. The beauty of an open class is, you never know who will show up. My teacher was doing the floor work on toe shoes while the rest of us labored in soft slippers. She was performing the most exquisite *fouette* turns, and then all of a sudden she went down in a crash. She seemed stunned and turned a tad red in the face, but was quickly back up on her feet. Our instructor asked her what happened and she said, "Oh, I don't know, my foot slipped inside of the shoe."

One never knows when the proverbial foot will slip in your shoe. It can happen anywhere, and there is no warning. There is nothing to prepare you for a fall that is in the offing. The ability to fall gracefully takes a certain temperament, but no one ever gets good at falling without training and preparing for it. "Life is not about waiting for the storm to pass, it's about learning how to dance in the rain" is a quote that is used often to inspire people; it is attributed to author and artist Vivian Greene.

To do little or nothing, far less than your professional best, means there will never be a reward for your efforts. Any time you pursue your best, you will be rewarded in some way, large or small, for your performance. In life and in business, we all go around in circles. We are hardwired to travel in orbit. How well we choose to travel is always at stake. How well will you travel around the circles that touch your lives?

There is always a reward inherent when you choose to explore excellence. And, *au contraire*, you can't be rewarded for doing the bare minimum, or just enough to get by, or in some cases, for doing nothing at all.

You can explore fall and recovery from all aspects of the circle. Whether you choose to do your best or not has no bearing on how many times you will go around in a circle. You will go around the same way as a *Rond de Jambé à terre*, the circling of the leg on the ground.

Once I worked with a woman who was extremely intelligent and well-educated. She often said she really liked her job, but she constantly made dumb mistakes out of simple carelessness and neglect. She never took initiative. She had a habit of making excuses for tasks that were left undone or had to be redone. She didn't listen to instructions. So I asked her to take notes. She was not receptive to feedback and bristled over this correction. In fact, any correction made her angry, which made matters worse. As much as I liked her, and found new ways for her to grow, I realized our standards were too different.

She made a habit of making mistakes and attributed them to being human. I understand being human, but I don't understand the habit of making mistakes. I was intent on performing at my highest level and considered a mistake to be a teachable moment—something to grow from and to learn to make a small adjustment—not something I would have to keep repeating. She was content to do the minimum just to get by, and I was on a mission to explore excellence. We would never be in alignment. By working for me, she represented my business and set the tone for its reputation. Our life philosophies were wildly out of sync and reflected poorly on my business, so I had to let her go.

When some people perform in business, they believe that what they are doing is great, even when it is mediocre. A trained mind knows when a performance isn't even close to being excellent. I think intense physical training over a sustained period of time gives you the ability to no longer try to fool yourself.

In the beginning when I first started training in ballet, the classes were held in studios with operating budgets too small to provide a live piano accompanist. Most of the music was provided by scratchy-sounding CDs in ancient players that had a tendency to skip, jam, reverberate strange tonal pitches, and stop working altogether. I have been in countless classes where the teacher spent more time trying to get a CD player going than teaching us ballet. Finally she would announce with great exasperation that we would just do the *Barré* without any music today.

I have taken classes where the pianist was a celebrated artist in his own right, and some where the pianist was a Russian woman, *Olga*, who complained that we did not keep up with her and then ran off early, leaving us with no music, so she could catch her bus. Another pianist, Harry, was a crackhead and an alcoholic. One night he was so drunk that he fell off the piano stool, but not before telling me that the teacher was the only person who was allowed to be blonde, and that I should take my own blondeness and leave the class.

Ballet also invites great emotional danger. Even though there are many reasons to dance, there are many obstacles that you will have to overcome. Ballet classes seem to draw as many extreme types of people as you find in the business world. And, the dysfunction and petty likes and dislikes among students in a class are the same as you experience in the business world.

I have often wondered if the professional dancers who dance beside us in class have any clue about the petty squabbles and rivalries that occur among the women who have no chance of dancing their way to fame or even of achieving professional standards. No one among the hobbyists is trying out to be cast as the next *Swan Queen*, and yet battles have erupted with the same fervor as mean girls and bullies in middle school. Sometimes the dance world is far more vicious than the business world! Martha Graham said, "Fire is the test of gold; adversity, of strong men."

The hardest thing I have experienced in ballet was seeing my daughter fall. Sarah has fallen many times. I cringe when she hits the ground. The other dancers in class are looking at me, wondering why I am not picking her up from the floor. There is nothing I can do. I know what she is feeling and my heart aches for her. She does not want me to make a fuss. She wants to get up from the floor as quickly as possible and with little fanfare. She has trick knees. A sign of remarkable flexibility, trick knees can be a good thing in ballet. She is building her muscle, the same way I have built my own muscle. Great flexibility requires great strength. Soon her knees will stop popping out.

Some students are not patient with the adult dancer who is in training for the first time. *Nellie* (not her real name) is sometimes in my class, and when I see her, I cringe with a touch of terror. With her long brown hair, parted in the middle and worn in a disheveled bun, she uses hippy lingo of the '60s and says things like *groovy*. She is in her 50s, and about 50 pounds overweight.

Out-of-shape and lacking form, she sweats profusely, and pants heavily like she's out of breath while she dances, but she always remembers the movements. She has had dance training in her past and regardless of what has happened to her body, the musicality comes back. Every time I saw her in class, she would take me to the side and whisper in a hoarse breath how I needed to mark my moves. "Mark it. Mark it. Mark it," she hissed at me. "Stand over here and mark it!" Nellie motioned me to the corner of the room like I was a naughty schoolgirl. It wasn't like I was bothering anyone. Somehow my inability to get the dance routine irritated her.

One summer day, I returned from vacation to take a class. The studio was hot, airless and felt like New York in the summer, but the mix and the vibe was neither urban nor upbeat. The air was thick with tension that had nothing to do with heat and humidity and little to do with the joy of dance.

Check out the line-up: there were serious hobbyists like me, who train consistently and take multiple classes every week. Then there were professional dancers, some from the corps, a couple of principal dancers, *stars*. Some of the professional dancers seemed to be coming back from injury. There were people from the beginning class who barely train once a week, if at all, and were clearly not prepared to be in a class with advanced dancers.

Even the *Barré* felt advanced, and it challenged me. I looked around the room and could see beginners who were looking dazed and lost, and losing their footwork.

This class, which was particularly difficult in all of its dynamics, was made even worse the moment I spotted Nellie. As soon as I saw her coming toward me, my heart sank. Everywhere in the room I went, she followed me. When I saw her coming, I went in the opposite direction. I had managed to avoid her for a while, until the moment when I could no longer escape. I had just gone across the floor. The line of dancers was jammed tight, body on top of body, pressed up against the back wall. Nellie came up to me and talked directly into my face. She was so close I could feel her hot, sour breath and see the beads of sweat dripping off her brow. She told me how beautiful and open my chest is, but how I am so uptight in my core. She went on a tirade about being uptight, and how unpleasant and offensive it is to watch, until I could no longer stand listening to her. I told her in a gentle *sotto voce* voice to *fuck off*.

A lot of people didn't make it through this class, which was more like boot camp for the Navy Seals than ballet. The beginners and most of the hobbyists didn't stay or try to do the floor work. This class was a futile exercise in dance. There was so little joy, and that made me sad somehow. Then I thought, would I have rather not have taken *any* class than to have taken *this* class? And I know that *any* dance class is better than *no* class. What did I learn? I can focus on what I am setting out to accomplish, no matter how many *Nellies* want to rip my bodice to shreds. If you think the business world can be ruthless, try ballet!

The great choreographer George Balanchine once said, "Most ballet teachers in the United States are terrible. If they were in medicine, everyone would be poisoned." And while I think this is somewhat of an exaggeration, I can say with certainty, after having experienced training with over thirty ballet teachers, a great teacher should make you feel that both of you are engaged in something truly exceptional. A great teacher will meet you where you are, and use her intuition and talent to guide you to take the next small, incremental change that will make you a better dancer. A great teacher will invest something of himself in you, and take pride and delight in seeing you improve.

There were classes where I did not literally fall but I did feel as though I suffered from a fall in grace. I have had some not-so-good experiences! Early in my training, I walked into a studio where the instructor told me it was obvious that I had some ballet training and asked me if I had been out of it for a while. Translation: *You are too old to dance.* When I first started taking classes in New York City, I found a small studio around Times Square. Every time I walked in, the guy who ran the studio told me, "You do know you have to have some training to take this class." In one class, the instructor stopped the class and spent thirty minutes talking about how upset she was because she didn't get a part in a Broadway show. Another time, a student who was a hot "Broadway star" thanked me for keeping up. I've been in classes where the teachers were obviously drunk, on drugs, or suffering from bouts of mental illness. One ballet instructor asked me to intervene with another dancer for being too aggressive with her space on the floor because she did not want to have to be the one to confront her.

The worst class I have taken was in New York City while I was there on business. For two years, I had seen dance legend David Howard at Steps on Broadway, in the hall outside the studios, sitting on the bench as if it was a long church pew. He always sat in the same spot on the bench, holding court with the many dancers who stopped to pay him homage. I admired his photo in which he was wearing a jaunty little cap perched on the side of his head. At one time he had his own ballet school, where the elite of the ballet world flocked to attend his classes: Baryshnikov, Gelsey Kirkland, Cynthia Harvey, and members of England's Royal Ballet, American Ballet Theatre, and the New York City Ballet.

David Howard taught his class from a walker. I didn't think the class was particularly advanced. It was an open class, meaning anyone could walk in to take the class, and was populated with dancers of all abilities, from the barely fluid and limber to a group of young male dancers, corps members, who were from the ABT. It was a Friday night, after a long week of business meetings. I remember feeling profound joy because my body was working fairly well. It was extremely hot. My body felt limber and I could do things. I could turn. I could jump. Throughout this class, David Howard had not said a word to anyone. He had not corrected anyone. He hardly seemed to be watching. He could not do anything, and could not demonstrate the steps he was asking us to implement. I found his style to be imperious, autocratic and old-school. Then we were doing a fairly complicated *adagio* across the floor. I went out in the first line just because I was there, already in position and ready to go. He suddenly bellowed to me, "You are not ready to go out front." So I just stopped and smiled due to sheer embarrassment. I wanted to talk back. I wanted to tell him if I was not ready now to go out in front, I would never be, but talking back is not *de rigueur* in ballet. I feared if I did say something, he would evict me from the class that I had paid nearly twenty dollars to attend.

As much as I tried to regain my composure during the rest of the class, I could not. I felt like I had been slapped around by a nun in Catholic school. The sting lingered, but I persevered and did the best I could do. The only thing I remember him saying was that "triples," meaning single pirouettes, were not enough. After class, when I walked into the hall, he gave me a huge grin. I did not know what that meant. Was it encouragement or an added jab of humiliation? Whatever it was, it did not feel good, and was contrary to all the reasons why I had practice ballet often enough to be able to do my best.

In the dressing room, I endured worse humiliation. "Susan" had bottle-black hair and appeared to be in her late 60s or older. She had been in the class with me, and it was obvious that she had not danced in a long time. The only people I focused on were the young male dancers, who were all excellent and had been dancing out front, where I was not supposed to be.

Susan complained to the women in the dressing room about "...a newcomer to the class who had walked in off the street as if she had seen one episode of 'Dancing with the Stars' and suddenly decided she would be a star." She was telling anyone who would listen that this newcomer had no right to be in the class. As I listened to her, I suddenly became mortified. Susan was talking about me!

Susan turned to me, shook her finger and accused me of having watched "Dancing with the Stars." Then she tore into me, insisting that I should not have been there because it was an advanced class. I told her I had read the schedule several times to make sure that it was listed as an *intermediate*, not an advanced, class. It may have been taught at an advanced level, but I had no way of knowing that. She asked me if I had ever taken a ballet class before. I calmly extended my leg and pointed my toe, and told her that one does not get such muscularity without consistently training. I had taken many classes, and this was not a good one. "In truth, it was one of the worst classes I have ever taken," I told her.

"You did not belong in that class. You have not trained!" Susan yelled. "It was a bad class," I said, pulling up my hose and stepping into my black pumps, "the worst class I've ever taken. He never corrected anyone." Susan yelled, "He does correct people! Sometimes," she spat out.

Another dancer who was listening chimed in. "David Howard is a mean-spirited person who only pays attention to stars. He only sucks up to doctors and lawyers because they can do something for him," the woman insisted. Then she turned to me. "David Howard used to teach a class in turning technique. I told him I would love to go to his class if only it was held earlier in the day, and do you know what he told me? He said, *I don't want you in my class."* I nodded with sympathy and pulled my shirt over my head. While I quickly stuffed my sodden tights and ballet slippers into a bag, Susan yelled at the woman, "David Howard is a star! He can run his class any way he wants!" The woman shot back, "Check out that photo of him in the hall. He's in the middle of a jump and his foot is sickled! He wasn't very good, even at the peak of his career!"

Before I kicked Susan in the head to show her the cumulative strength of many hours of dance training, I hightailed it out of there into the hot, humid night onto Broadway, where I ducked into the subway station. I had looked forward to going to a class with a teacher I had not met before, where I would be anonymous and the community would be new and fresh, only to stumble upon a bad dance scene. If I want to go out in front, even if I'm not ready, it's my choice. I'm a student who is paying for a class. I'm not a professional dancer trying out for a part in an audition.

The embarrassment stayed with me until the next day. I felt humiliated because his proclamation was not a correction, but a put-down. Susan was a *David Howard* groupie, albeit an old one, who was filled with an uncommon bitterness and over-the-top rage. I thought of quitting dance, but it was only a momentary feeling. After all, I know that above and beyond all of my foibles and weaknesses, the one thing that is true and real—I know how to climb steps.

The next morning, I took a train to Boston to attend to a private family matter. On the trip, I passed the ruins of factories that looked like twisted metal skeletons, hunks of iron fossils, industrial debris, broken tools and relics from another era, amid huge mountains of hubcaps. I saw the rusted carcasses of freight cars, the entrails of containerized cargo, and new clapboard housing developments where there were no signs of human life. Fields were filled with massive rows of high-tension power lines and mounds of wrecked, rusted and flattened cars looking like the graveyards of old energy. I saw small muddied ponds and an enormous parking lot full of big yellow schoolbuses. One large trainyard was full of renewable containers marked RRMG *Renewable Rounds Marketing Group*—large liquid containers thinly disguised by the ominous logo *RRMG* —as if you did not know they were full of toxic waste.

Each passing town had an abandoned church, worn down to its foundation of stone and brick. Old cemeteries with crumbling tombstones and faded names were decorated with little flags and dried-out flower bouquets left over from Memorial Day. More than old churches, factories and junkyards, I was seeing the final entrails of a lost way of life, life before technology and the Internet. And even though the churches were dying or gone, I am still moving forward and finding a way to believe in something. In this changing world, dance has been a constant star, a vital force to count on and to give me the experience to trust myself. I felt like I could reach out and touch the leaves of the branches of trees almost gliding against the side of the train like a *glissade*.

I started to see David Howard as an old, bitter fossil who had lost his joy for dance. Although he was very much into the *lifestyle of dance,* a principal or player in the culture of the dance world, I began to refer to him as *the dinosaur of dance*. He was from another time and another world, the same as an old factory ruin or an abandoned church. He might be a dance legend and have an incredible reputation among some of the world's greatest classical dancers, but I will only remember the lasting impression he made on me. I learned a powerful lesson: ultimately, you are in charge of your own brand legacy. Every little thing you say or do affects how you will be remembered.

Aspiring to do your best personally and professionally always invites emotional and physical danger. Ironically, not to aspire to excellence also invites the same risk of danger. I can't tell you if my desire to do my professional best is born out of some early psychological trauma or is simply a matter of genetic hard-wiring. I don't think it is a family trait; most of the family members I have known were happy enough to settle for less. They did not take a risk by going outside the narrow ken spanning eight blocks from St. Mary's Church to Getty Square in Yonkers.

On one trip back east, I wanted to take my grandmother out to dinner one night. I drove into Manhattan, intending to take her to one of my favorite restaurants, *La Bibliotheque* in Tudor City, which had a small outdoor café that looked out to the UN and the East River. We never got there. She was very uncomfortable and had little to say in the car. Grandmother was out of her milieu and not handling change well. Finally, I could not bear seeing her squirm any longer, turned the car around and took her home. We went instead to her favorite Italian restaurant, *Louie's* on South Broadway, which was within walking distance of her home on Jackson Street.

During the past five years, I have logged many hours of ballet training without a serious injury. There have been little kinks and pulls and sore muscles, but nothing that required medical intervention.

The largest physical fall I took was when I danced with a giant wedding cake. My daughter Katie was married in the summer and in her rapid departure to start her honeymoon, her massive red velvet wedding cake was forgotten. As our usually moderate Seattle summer days heated up to the high 90s, the cake was melting, dripping icing everywhere. So I shoved the dissolving cake into my large freezer, where it remained for six months. If only I knew then what I know now: no one *ever* wants to eat leftover wedding cake!

January is my month to purge all rich food, frozen or not,

from the house. So although there was slush on the streets, I heaved this enormously dense wedding cake into a large trash bag and started down the icy steps. I was slipping and sliding, and the cake was rolling back on top of me. I knew I was in trouble, so I lunged forward and tossed it to the sidewalk as if it was a *discus*. Now the cake sat quivering in the garbage bag on top of new-fallen snow.

I reached down, picked up the cake and catapulted forward. My open arms were outstretched, holding onto the cake. I had great technique: Legs turned out, knees slightly bent in a *demi-plié* in fourth position. Then my strong feet slid forward in the slush, skidding and slipping while the cake overtook me. Just as the cake reached the top of the garbage can and easily slid in, it carried me along with it as if I was an unwilling partner, sheer dead weight in a tragic *pas de deux*. I felt a pull in my back, nothing more than a slight twinge. But the next day it was so painful, I could hardly walk. I had injured my lower left lumbar. I'd like to say that it happened while I was in class, dancing or working out vigorously. At least then I could say I went down heroically, but no such luck. All the right training in the world can leave you totally unprepared for that unexpected mishap. But when you think about it, in ballet, women never do the heavy lifting.

There are many times when I fell while I was doing something other than practicing ballet. One night I was on a walk with my husband. A long spiraling coil-like wire jutted out from a utility pole and caught on my shoe, tripping me. I jettisoned forward in a free fall, but my feet responded quickly almost as if I was practicing a *petite allegro* and, instead of hitting the ground, I jumped in the air and regained my footing. Another time, the tip of my shoe hit the jagged rut of pavement in a slab of sidewalk that was pushed up from the earth by the roots of a tree. I went free-falling forward, but quickly regained my footing and came back to center.

Annie de Vuono is fond of telling her students that rarely

will they injure themselves in the studio while they are dancing. Dancers may be out and about, doing something completely unrelated to dance, when they have an unforeseeable accident. For example, one day I took a full-court ballet class at PNB in the morning, and jumped out of a plane in the afternoon, skydiving. The next morning I went out to the garden to water my roses and twisted my ankle on a stepping stone. *Lack of focus.* Not being here and not being present. Maybe if I had focused on the roses instead of allowing my thoughts to race ahead to the next thing, I wouldn't have twisted my ankle. And yet ballet teaches you to be here, one foot on the ground, the other leaping toward the next steps, and to future movements, a bit like having one foot on the ground and another foot leaping toward heaven.

The twist to my ankle was slight. I was back in Pilates class the next day and in ballet class the second day. During the times when I have taken a fall, my muscle tone and balance was so strong due to ballet training that I quickly rebounded with little or no injury.

Barbara Willis is the dancer and instructor who teaches Parkinson's patients to dance as a way to celebrate life and to minimize the progression of the disease they are afflicted with. She works closely with Dr. Brian Grabert, a neurologist at Colorado Springs Health Partners. He treats about 200 Parkinson's patients, including Barbara Willis and some of the people who train in her dance program. "In general," Dr. Grabert said, "those who exercise appear more upbeat and less apathetic, and they tend to report having fewer falls, one of the most serious consequences of the disease as it progresses." It was observed that despite having Parkinson's disease, *Barbara Willis moves with the steady grace you might expect from someone who's taught dance for decades.**

---

* Controlled Moves Sun Journal June 28 2009
http://www.newbernsj.com/articles/disease-46186-parkinson-willis.html

Professional ballet dancers are able to do with their bodies what only a few of us are able to do with our minds. These dancers embody the best of athleticism, technical training, lyricism, artistry, and experience. They have spent their entire lives becoming professional dancers. There is a wide chasm between those of us who will never dance professionally because we are not strong enough and those who are so good they cannot afford to make a mistake. When you are a professional, you do not have the luxury of falling often. Most of the time you have to hit your marks. If not, there is a price to pay.

Why do I dance? It may be my inability to attain the ideal that makes my ballet training so much more engaging. I am mesmerized by the possibility that the next class I walk into, I will do one small thing to make me dance better than I danced the last time. I am not so much striving to be good in ballet as I am striving to be the best possible businessperson, wife, lover, mother, friend, writer and all the other myriad of activities that I find myself engaged in. It also means that every now and then, I must take a hard fall.

Many of us don't have the luxury of engaging in a passion or a part-time pursuit that will hone our skills enough so we can learn how to fall gracefully. And yet if you want to pursue excellence, you must find a way to practice the art of falling and recovery. Whether you are a dancer or a dilettante, a business person, a creative professional, a performing artist, an academic, an author or an athlete, you have to give yourself controlled and disciplined opportunities to fall so you can explore a higher level of excellence.

Some of us fear giving it our all. If you hold back one small thing, then if you should fail or not perform quite to your expectations, you can always say, I didn't really give it my all. No one can criticize your performance if you were not dancing full-out.

Actress Shirley MacLaine attributes her many years of dance

training to giving her a sense of stability within the core of her being. "[Some people are] searching for those highs, and desperate when they reach those lows," she says. "That doesn't happen to me anymore. It never did much. I was too stable for that, thanks to my training as a dancer. It's sort of like what the Buddhists say: Do the middle way. It's like a violin. Don't stretch it too tight or it will break, and don't let it too loose or you won't have any music. I've got all these things stored up, these little secrets about life."*

Fall and recovery is akin to being banished from the Garden of Eden. You have to take the risk of temptation. You're human. You have to try something new and take a bite from the apple. You have to fail. Sooner or later, you will fall. You will be banished from paradise, and on the day that you are banished, you will learn something about yourself that you did not know before now. You will be given great grace. Ironically, you can't be given grace until you are banished from paradise.

I think of all the times I am on the verge of falling, and the terror of being in that space where I am about to fall. Try moving backward and not being able to see where you are going. More than any other teacher I have had, Bruce Wells at PNB frequently trains us to move backward. This is when he uses his time-worn phrase, *The river runs back*. Then you know you are moving backward. It's scary to dance backward when you cannot see where you are going. You begin to trust your instincts. You begin to have faith in your body. You can feel the other dancers moving around you. The river runs back, and so do I. Without looking down to the floor or to either side, I am dancing backward. I am feeling the river coursing through my veins with the quiet natural rhythm of life.

---

* Shirley MacLaine on life, showbiz and finding contentment By Moira Macdonald Seattle Times June 12, 2010 http://seattletimes.nwsource.com/html/movies/2012073537_shirley13.html

The river runs back brings you to a place you have been to before, and now you are looking at it in a wholly different way. Every time you revisit a memory, it is always a little different than the last time. With this power of recollection, you begin to have a sense of knowing yourself a little better than you ever have before you stepped into this place in time and traced back this memory to another time in your life. And this is why I keep returning to the steps in my grandmother's house.

The last time I saw my grandmother Katherine, she was in a nursing home. The old tenement at 67 Jackson Street was long gone and a graffiti-scrawled, high-rise, low-income, housing project stood in its place. For most of my grandmother's adult life, she had done volunteer work every day at St. Joseph's Hospital. The hospital and the nursing home were located within the same eight-block radius between Getty Square and St. Mary's Church.

Now, during her final days, she was locked down in an Alzheimer's ward at St. Joseph's Hospital.

Grandmother's eyes, a startling shade of blue, flickered with recognition when she saw me. She was wearing a pink sweatshirt and sweatpants. Her silver hair was done in a sleek pageboy with short bangs. She told me she had just jogged around the running track, round and round the track. She was so proud of her physical feat. She always carried herself with great pride as well as great humility. And this time was no exception. Pride and humility appear to be a contradiction, but when they co-exist within the same person, one seems to balance the other, and the person becomes imbued with great grace. Just like the classic *Rond de Jambé*, my grandmother was going around the circle and learning until the very last days of her life.

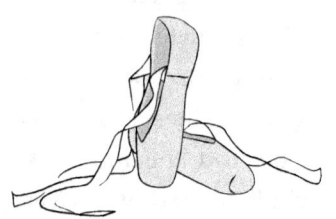

— 8 —

Hitting Your Marks

I can never forget the steps inside my grandmother's home in the tenement at 67 Jackson Street in South Yonkers. I recall the faded turquoise color and the uneven, jagged shape of the steps. The steps were old, worn and steep, and as much as I climbed them, they always proved dangerous. I could lose my footing and skin my shin or twist my ankle. But it never happened. I became so good at climbing these steps that I hit my marks.

Years later, when my daughter Katie was in kindergarten on the monkey bars, she became a champion climber in her own right. The mother of a little boy who was Katie's friend told me her son wanted to marry Katie. When his mother asked him why, he responded with his own rhetorical question. He said to his mother, "Have you seen her climb?"

The last time I saw my grandmother, she was in the nursing home. She told me she had run the outdoor track, not once, but many times. Her eyes twinkled with Irish mirth—a combination of pride and mischief. Later on, the nurses told me she had not run the track at all. In fact, she had not been outdoors for days. Remember, she was in the Alzheimer's ward and it was locked down. No one got in or out of the ward without going through checkpoints. In her mind, though, grandmother believed she had been running. And in some ways, she had indeed run the entire course.

Hitting your marks is a metaphysical pursuit that touches every aspect of life and business. As you might have guessed, I regard business as a celebration of life. There is something uplifting and spiritual about doing what you are good at doing, and in turn, receiving some form of compensation. The compensation can be money, barter or a psychic reward. The essence of this transaction is a spiritual exchange, a give-and-take, a transfer of energy from one person or thing to another. This thing called business is all about life. And wanting to explore excellence is a way of extending one's self to reach for a higher ideal, to be a little better as a human being than you were yesterday.

In ballet, no matter what level you attain, you learn about *holding your head up*. I remember one class I took the day before Easter Sunday. It was one of those Seattle days with full sun and the blue sky of paradise. The ornamental cherry trees were in full bloom. There were daffodils and tulips everywhere, poking up from the ground like the heads of proud little people. Sarah and I took Annie de Vuono's class. Afterward, we had another hour and a half of rehearsal. Annie had developed a new mantra. When we were doing a particularly challenging sequence with lots of turns and jumps, she announced, "Let's perfect this sucker." We worked really hard in class and did our best to move toward perfection, easier said than done.

Spencer had returned to class. I remember how he started training with Annie a couple of years ago, when he was 15, and then moved on to PNB. Now he is going to the Pennsylvania State Ballet as a company member.

Annie has a special gift for inspiring people. "Rachel" is a very tall and beautiful dancer. She said she now holds her head up higher while she is dancing because Annie taught her how to use the magnificence of her height. We should all learn to hold our heads up. No matter what is going on, even if the world is falling apart all around us, holding our heads high is what gives us the ability to press on and to explore excellence.

The adrenalin of being engaged in business takes me out of myself. I am not dwelling on small obstacles and getting stuck. Business and dance are two pursuits that require the dedication and discipline to spur on activity in order to achieve a remarkable "lightness of being."

You have heard of the work + family + lifestyle balance, which suggests you must arrange your life in compartments and separate your work from the other aspects of your life. But that will only make you miserable. You cannot divide your work + family + lifestyle as if it is a pie, and you are giving away slices of time. You are your work, and you should love your work passionately enough to call it your life. And it should touch upon everything you say and do.

There is something very healthy about commerce taking place. Bartering, buying and selling, all the forces that drive a market economy are thrilling, full of action and vitality, and help to sustain life. Hitting your marks in business means your style, your skills, your experience, all derived through training and discipline, plus your level of commitment, all merge at the same time and arrive together in the same place. Hitting your marks is not always possible, but it's impossible to realize a dream if you don't put in the necessary hard work.

Modern dance pioneer Doris Humphrey believed that the dancer could express things in his art that could not be expressed in any other way. *"There are times when the simple dignity of movement can fulfill the function of a volume of words. There are movements which impinge upon the nerves with a strength that is incomparable, for movement has power to stir the senses and emotions, unique in it. This is the dancer's justification for being, and his reason for searching further for deeper aspects of his art."*

And so it goes when you train to dance. You come to know that you will keep going around the circle of the *Rond de Jambé* to rise higher within your own self. In ballet, you will explore the full range of movement, from the *grande allegro* to the most subtle positioning of your hand or foot. In the discovery and heightened awareness of your physical body, you also come to know in precise detail who you are as a person. Martha Graham said, "Nothing is more revealing than movement."

Steps is an ongoing lesson in grace. You are moving forward, one step at a time, whether they are balletic steps, or business steps building your brand, the story of *Steps* is one of risk and calculated chance. It means no matter what happens to you, you will always feel compelled to climb higher. Your mission is to move the people whom you touch through your compassion, beauty, elegance, dedication and hard work. We are all sharing the same human experience, and we all have a need to elevate ourselves to a higher level. We are moved. We care. We are human. We can reach to find a better place in ourselves.

Barbara Willis is a dancer who has Parkinson's disease; she teaches other Parkinson's patients to dance. "For an hour each week, they march, they balance, they dance back and forth to music, all with the idea that they can use movement to combat a disease infamous for taking it away. Some of their caregivers also participate. The aim of the class is to try to move as beautifully as you can."*

If you come to know who you are as a person, you should have great pride coupled with great humility, which is worn like an old cloak as a reminder of embracing all you are in order to rise higher. It is by traversing this circle that you learn about

---

* Controlled Moves Sun Journal June 28 2009
http://www.newbernsj.com/articles/disease-46186-parkinson-willis.html

your life and live your destiny. You become the person that you were meant to be.

I have too much humility to call myself a dancer. I have been in the same studios with great dancers and have come to know and embrace their aesthetic ideal. I myself am a woman who trains as a dancer so I can be better at all other important aspects of my life.

In the ballet world, there is a tradition of famous teachers mentoring their soon-to-be-famous students with the grandeur and authority of God, or George Balanchine. I recall when I was taking a class given by Julie Tobiason, who recalled her experiences training with the legendary muse and Balanchine's wife, Maria Tallchief. Gelsey Kirkland recently started up the Gelsey Kirkland Academy of Classical Ballet so she could mentor students in a method that could not be replicated in other ballet schools. Even teachers who never had a career in dance still extol the virtues of their teachers. Elaine Bonow, from a small studio in Belltown, used to sing praises of Irene Larsson, a relatively unknown teacher who long ago taught at The Academy of Classic Ballet in Seattle.

The way ballet instructors share the stories of their own training is similar to the stories we tell about ourselves, in business and elsewhere. These stories, ever-evolving and changing, are told through what we say and what we write: your articles, books and press releases, on websites and blogs, and through videos. These stories are covered by the press when they write about you. These stories are told when other people talk you up on social media. Ballet teachers don't just teach a class, they hand down a legacy of training by telling little anecdotes about the things their teachers told them.

Storytelling builds your brand. Every word you say should be a tribute to you and your brand, who you are and how you want others to remember you. How will you get your name known? How will you build your legacy? How do you want to be remembered?

When I return to the steps on 67 Jackson Street, I remember the last night I saw my grandmother. She showed me old photos of relatives; few are living and most have passed. She also showed me letters written by my *great-great-grandmother* Katherine O'Toole to her daughter, my *great-grandmother* Mary Mulqueen. Beautifully hand-lettered and worded with care and sensitivity, they were odes to her daughter Mary, telling her how much she missed her. Mary had left Ireland and moved to America. The letter was stamped with the name Elamura, a tiny town in County Galway. Later, Mary had six children, one of whom was my grandmother Katherine. Two of Mary's youngest children died in a *"pesthouse,"* where sick children were sent and quarantined during the Great Influenza Epidemic of the early 20th century. "Oh, my Mary, I miss you so," Katherine wrote, mourning for her daughter as if she would never see her again. And given the times they lived in, Mary was indeed gone forever.

I was surprised to learn that my *great-great-grandmother* could write well. I always return to those steps on Jackson Street, where I learned of her letters from Elamura. A fourth-grade teacher told me I had a gift for writing. So over time, it never surprised me to know that writing was a major part of my life and my business—my destiny. Ballet training has touched every aspect of my life, personally and professionally, and has enhanced my work as a professional writer; I always have to hit high standards in my writing, whether I feel like it or not. In my business, I typically write an average of 10,000 words a week, all subject to client approval or scrutiny by the public and the press. This form of writing is called production writing.

The hardest part about hitting your marks is the process

of letting go and losing something you have worked hard to create. The hardest part about writing is having to let go of sentences, sometimes passages and whole pages that you really love, because by removing them, the work as a whole will be stronger and more profound. The same is true in dance—it is hard to lose a step that the dancers are not getting or that is not adding to the fluidity or the meaning of the piece. The same holds true in business. You decide to lose a product, a service, an employee, a client, or a communication style. These are hard decisions, not to be made by the unexercised, the undisciplined or the inexperienced.

Going around the circle to explore excellence is not the pursuit of perfection. Perfection will never be good enough. Perfection will never give you the creative freedom to make mistakes. It is only by taking risks and by making mistakes that we are able to explore excellence. We also learn a certain discernment. Sometimes we can't give a work or a project our absolute best. We only do what is necessary to get the job done. Hitting our marks also means taking the right number of steps at the right time. For example, if I'm on deadline to write a press release or an article, then I'm going to give it my professional best, but I'm not going to put in the time to take it up to the level of a literary masterpiece. Writing to hit an eternal or literary standard is another process altogether. This form of writing is meant to stand the test of time, and so each passage must be rigorously rewritten, pondered and polished.

The longer you spend time training in dance, the more you come to know when to keep going and to persevere. You also come to know when the time comes to quit. The energy flow of knowing when to persevere, or knowing when to quit, is a great metaphor for business. You develop the intuition of knowing when to stay the course and press on, and when to come to a complete stop, and find a new direction.

Having a gift for auditory perfection, Bruce Wells at PNB uses his beautiful phrases to teach us ballet. I've mentioned his phrase *The river runs back* to describe when we are moving backward and dancing in the opposite direction, and also how, throughout a class, many times he will say, *Eyes up*. And how, after a time while you are dancing, you become aware that your eyes are always tilting upward. Dance becomes a powerful meditation, almost a prayer, to climb higher. When you are exploring excellence in business, the time comes when you must raise the *Barré* to take you and your work to the highest level you can attain.

Writers have a special method for hitting their marks. Don DeLillo is an author who grew up in the Bronx. His work paints a detailed portrait of American life in the late 20th and early 21st centuries. According to an article in the *Wall Street Journal*, "His approach to writing borders on obsessive. He fixates on the shapes of letters and words, and judges each phrase for its visual appearance as well as its rhythm and clarity. "

His editor at Scribner's noted that Don DeLillo likes to use word combinations where one word surrounds another, such as "raw sprawl."

Don DeLillo noted that sometimes he will swap out a word for a more rhythmically appealing one, even if it alters the meaning of the sentence. He often types up a single paragraph at a time, using a clean sheet of paper for each paragraph, so that he can study the architecture of each passage in isolation.*

I understand his magnificent obsession with the written word. Gifted writers never really finish a piece unless they have to turn it in on deadline.

My training as an adult dancer has taught me that writing is

---

* What Don DeLillo's Books Tell Him by Alexandra Alter, WSJ, Jan 30 2010
http://online.wsj.com/article/SB10001424052748704094304575029673526948334.html

one more place to explore excellence. You who are writers care about writing and writing well. You know and understand that there can be no clear writing without clear thought. Writers are the protectors of thought. When you're working, engaged in the process of writing, once you have established your clear thought, you know how hard you must work to elevate your writing to the next level, where you must strive to attain the rhythm, elegance and beauty of language. This process is part talent, part skill, part experience, part alchemy and sometimes sheer luck. You are, after all, a wordsmith.

The novelist Annie Dillard likens writing a book to keeping a feral beast that must be visited daily if the writer is to preserve mastery over it. "If you skip a day, you are, quite rightly, afraid to open the door to its room." A writer works with words the same disciplined way a dancer trains to stay in shape. I think you might feel the way I feel about writing, dance, business and life. I approach them all with a certain awe and reverence. Writing, dancing, business, life; these are a few of the things that, when I am doing any one of them, I do not feel that I should be doing anything else in the world.

One Friday, I drove to Annie de Vuono's morning class. It was a classic Seattle spring day, gray and overcast. The only way you could tell that we were on the verge of summer was the abundance of greenery. Our evergreens are perpetual all year long, but now all the other trees had sprung thick canopies of leaves. The daffodils and tulips had shed their petals and died back to stalks. Peonies were blooming, and lilies were shooting up from the ground.

This ballet class was like any other. I can't recall making a breakthrough. In fact, I can't really recall any class when I did make a breakthrough. I can't identify a class when I learned how to do a *pique* turn or my first *pirouette*. I would do one competent pirouette, then six lousy ones. Then I would do two or three decent pirouettes, and only one bad turn. I was always taking two steps forward and one step back.

After class, my teacher Annie de Vuono told me that I had found my place on the floor. I had been training for five years, and I guess it was finally starting to show. I didn't feel any grand emotion like pride or elation; I felt imbued with great humility and a sense of grace. I could only think of how much work I had left to do.

I can't tell you how much work it took to get to this point. There are as many small victories as there are small failures. There is a profound exuberance derived from dance that is like no other form of joy I have known, except for the exhilaration you feel in every phase of romantic love. The first flush of new love will leave you breathless; like dance, over time that feeling develops into the deep certainty that you have been given a gift. You have been given a profound sense of knowing yourself.

You own the ability to explore excellence in your own self with as much form and discipline as a great ballet dancer.

Building your brand and your business means you will manage them indefinitely—for the rest of your life. You really don't ever take a day off. And why should you want a day off? You want to let the world know who you really are. You are essentially what you choose to say and who you say it to, every single person or situation that you encounter. You are always conscious of what you stand for and how you will express it, to everyone from the checkout clerk in the grocery store to the CEO of a Fortune 500 company.

Every ballet dancer learns to be technically proficient in a vast number of steps. Of course there are different training methods between *Vaganova* and *Cechetti* schools, and I have noticed distinct difference in the instruction between my American teachers and their Russian or Eastern European counterparts. And yet with all of the differences, a professional ballet dancer must achieve a high level of technical competence in order to get roles, to achieve ascendancy or prominence in the hierarchical rank of the corps or company, and finally, just to get paid to dance. So while there is a standard for technical competence, after that it is all about the unique personality of the dancer. Each dancer's personality, education, training, artistry, physical athleticism has special attributes that are inherently her own.

One day I was in an open class taught by Alexandra Dickson. She gave each of us varied levels of correction. For me, correction meant not to sickle my foot or to notice how expansively I held my arms. Another, more advanced dancer was given a correction of the proper extension of her arms while she was in *Arabesque*. There was one exquisite dancer, who was obviously a professional. Alexandra complimented her form and her performance, and said, "Now I want you to dance as if you own it. Bring the depth of your personality to the movement." She was being guided to bring her unique attributes to the piece, to take ownership, and to embody her brand as a dancer.

If you want to explore excellence, then you need to be working at the same level as professionals. Whether you are building a business or managing your brand, with the right training you can act like a professional. For example, if you want success, there are certain things you need to do to hit your marks.

You need to know your own story, who you are and why your story is different from all other stories. Your story needs to be fun, clever, original, and, above all else, true. You need to tell the story to the audiences that you want to reach. You need to sustain the telling of the story over a long period of time. You need to keep telling the same story with different twists and turns, plots and characterization, with new angles and adding on episodes, addendums and sequels. You are weaving a spell. You are creating magic. You are making an emotional connection and bonding with your audience. Your story is simple, but as complicated and as challenging as achieving balance in your *Promenade*.

Destiny. Each of you is dealt a certain hand in cards. Your talents, your gifts, your skills, your appearance, your scent, your voice, your style, and your preferences: your likes and dislikes, your beliefs and your experiences, all of these things are uniquely you. You may not be destined to be a royal princess or the next President of the United States. Often, you may be driven by forces other than your pursuit to be who you really are because you are trying to please someone else: a parent, a spouse or a boss. Perhaps you are denying some aspect of yourself that you do not understand. You keep hitting your head against the wall. The façade isn't working. You get physically sick, tired or depressed. You keep getting stonewalled or blocked from your goals. Whenever you try to be who you are not, it is the same as donning a mask to cover your real face. "You are unique, and if that is not fulfilled, then something has been lost," Martha Graham said.

I love dance in the same way that I love my business. From day to day, I never know for sure whether I am making the right business decision. I am operating on a combination of feeling (intuition) and experience (training). It is the same way with dance. It is only recently that can I move across the floor and execute a whole series of complicated steps. Before I *glissade* across the floor, I feel a sense of doubt, uncertainty and fear. Are my feet pointed? Will I make a *sauté* with a straight working leg? Am I pulling up straight in my torso during my turns? Is my *passé* turned out enough? Will I remember every step? Will my fluidity and form be a bit more improved than it was yesterday? Will today be the day when I finally do a *fouette* turn?

Whenever you are exploring excellence, you will encounter challenges, setbacks and failures. You could also be on the wrong road and encounter all the same challenges, setbacks and failures. It is hard to distinguish true obstacles from the signs that you are on the wrong road. So how do you know what is right for you? How do you know if you are following your destiny?

You know you are on the wrong road when doors keep slamming in your face and new doors do not open. You are forced to wander in the desert with no respite in sight. Things keep going wrong. Accidents and mishaps keep happening. You know you are doing everything right, but the outcome always turns out wrong. Author Caroline Schoeder said, "Some people change when they see the light, others when they feel the heat."

You know you are following your destiny when new doors keep opening up. Even though you struggle with adversity, the small wins and little victories keep telling you that you are on the right road. Somehow the opening of each new door transforms you, shaping and defining your character a little more sharply. Suddenly it becomes apparent that the road you are on is not really a road at all. Instead, you are taking a journey to learn how you can best serve yourself with integrity. And by serving yourself, you serve the world. As Willa Cather suggests: "The end is nothing, the road is all."

Since you are you, why would you want to be anything other than who you are destined to be? It is your mission to explore who you really are. You have a destiny to fulfill what is unique and exceptional about you. You may offer unique qualities or services, or unique products and goods. You need to convey to your community just how good you are at what you do and how useful you can be. Life is too short not to learn who you are and to enjoy everything that you can offer to the world. The only way to achieve lasting fulfillment and success is to be certain of who you really are.

Now there is no stopping you. Take one step. One step at a time. You are moving. You are beginning to dance. You are soaring for the sky. You are dancing. Everywhere you go, you are exploring excellence. Gelsey Kirkland said the one thing dancers have to learn on their own that no one can teach them is, "Sacrifice. The desire to explore. You can inspire that, but you cannot teach it." *

I have come to know *Dance as the physical articulation of a song. Dance is losing one's self and knowing one's self: submission and complete mastery, one and the same. Of only one thing I am certain: when you are learning to dance, nothing else in the world seems hard or impossible.* If you can dance, you can see that all other things are easy by comparison. The choreographer Doris Humphrey said, "When we move we stand revealed for what we are."

After many years of wondering what had happened to my childhood friend Carmen Canavan, one day she found me. She sent me an email and then we spoke by phone. Her voice was still lyrical and unaccented. She had lived in London for a time, married, and started a ballet school. She no longer dances. She had changed her name from Carmen to *Juliette,* and despite the name change, I still think of her as Carmen. On the dance floor, her brown eyes were huge and she leapt like a gentle fawn. I remember her lilting expressions and the way her hands fluttered in the air while she spoke. I haven't yet caught up with her. I still hold the image I know of her from our youth. Soon, when I return to New York, I will see her. I will let you know how it turns out. We are two women who have lived a whole lifetime apart from one another, and only share a common connection in dance. Ted Shawn, a pioneer of American modern dance, said, "Dance is the only art in which we ourselves are the stuff of which it is made."

---

* Straight from the heart: Gelsey Kirkland looks back ... and ahead
Dance Magazine, Sept. 2005 by Kate Lydon

Otto Compane Concerto in A minor for Violin by Bach was performed on May 14, 2011, at Broadway Performance Hall. The eight bells have let go and I can only speak in images. We are in the green room, warming up. Sarah is stretching her leg in full extension. Behind her, five hip-hop dancers are standing backward, facing an outside window, warming up. They are doing these cool moves and marking. In the foreground, Sarah is holding her extension. She is unaware of them and they are unaware of her. Everyone is warming up in their own space, oblivious to what the other dancers are doing. The full extension of Sarah's leg crosses over, courses through the air and intersects across the image of the hip-hopping backs. Everyone is in their own space. How incredible it is to see Sarah's fully extended balletic leg, the hip-hop dancers in the background moving flawlessly, like dancing wallpaper. I see the image so clearly in my mind. My daughter has climbed high enough to reach her own space on the floor.

Then we are in the wings, waiting to take the stage. Our performance whisks by, in a blur faster than the speed of light. We walk offstage and back into the green room. Everyone is a tad self-critical. We talk about what we messed up: one little tweak here, one misstep there, a forgotten move and a shaky turn. I didn't do a high enough *relevé* in *arabesque*, but I hit my marks. I think my timing was fast, but I love the way my adrenaline kicked in and took me up to a level I did not know I had inside of myself until now. There is an exuberance that accompanies a feeling of letting go. I will remember this, dancing with my daughter, all the days of my life.

The performance was, in many ways, anti-climactic. It was the process, getting here; all of the afternoons we had talked about life and other things, in rehearsal, dancing together, knowing one another in a way we had never known before, growing apart, coming together again, *the river runs back*. While we danced together, I witnessed my child become a woman. I was the child who climbed steps. How I wish I had the chance to dance with my mother! And now my child has danced with me. She, too, has learned how to climb steps. Sarah and I are here together, in the dance of the pink snow.

I never said goodbye to my grandmother Katherine. I was the only grandchild, who did not stop by to see her before she passed. I lived 3,000 miles away. In some ways, I feel like I did not know her. She lost both of her younger sisters to the Great Influenza Epidemic; Josephine was a toddler, and Mary was an infant. Her mother, my great-grandmother, doted on Katherine because she was the last living daughter. Some people say that's why Simon started drinking. Little Josephine used to stand in the window every night and wait for him to come home from work. When the window went dark, he could not live with the grief.

My grandmother Katherine had an enduring childlike quality that made her too fearful to venture beyond the narrow ken of her neighborhood. I always felt she had not become inspired enough to climb her own steps. There was no escaping the sadness in the walls of her old tenement. She had suffered the loss of her sisters. Oh, and there were other losses, too. Her daughter. Her son. These are other stories to tell someday.

Had I stayed in New York, I would have fought to win back the old tenement. There are days when I still remember what it was like to live there. If the place was mine, I could fix it up and live there again. There was something magical about a home with steps that climbed to the sky.

Very few human beings are struck with the force of a thunderbolt and experience the whole truth in a single moment of clarity. Most people learn the truth in one small increment at a time, by spiraling up and down a hidden staircase that speaks to their soul, and by taking steps. "Art is the only way to run away without leaving home," Twyla Tharp said.

Until I started dancing, I had not thought about my grandmother Katherine for many years. Then one night, many years after her death, she came to me in a dream. I walked into the old brown tenement and found her in the kitchen, sitting at a small white-enameled steel table. Although it was dark, everything could be seen clearly and there were no shadows. It was the blue hour, first crack of dawn, before you can see the sun rise in the sky. There is neither full daylight nor complete darkness—what the French call *l'heure bleue*.

Grandmother explained to me that the electricity had been turned off. She did not understand why her electricity had been turned off, especially when she had always paid her bill on time. She said developers had come by and offered her a price, but she could not sell the tenement because she did not have the deed. She wouldn't be able to live there without heat in the winter. She was going to stay there a few more days and then move out. She was looking forward to moving and getting new furniture. She told me that she was glad I had come home for a visit. I told her I would carry the steps with me everywhere. "Everywhere I go, I climb," I said. She nodded and smiled. I could see her blue eyes shining in the soft gray light, as if she knew something I did not know.

"Every dance is a kind of fever chart, a graph of the heart," said Martha Graham. In my own mind, when I dance in my head, I am far better than I am out on the real dance floor. I am dancing from my heart, which is no small thing. In my mind, I dance for my husband, because he is the other half of my soul. He thinks dance is a way for me to empower my own beauty that runs deep beneath my skin. I dance for my daughter Sarah, because she is often there dancing with me. She stretches and extends, bending and growing like a willow tree. I dance for my son David, because I think it gives him hope that we can accomplish anything with our mind that we resolve to do. I dance for my daughter Katie, because I want her to see all the things in life that are possible. I dance for my father, because even though he is long gone, I imagine there is a place called heaven where he can see me, and the sight of his daughter dancing gives him great joy. I dance for my mother, because I know if she could see me, she would smile. I dance for my grandmother Katherine. She is the dance in my heart that will not stop dancing.

Seattle can be a strange and wonderful place in the spring. The temperature is often in the high 40s by night and the low 50s by day, the same as it was in January. The only way you know that you are transitioning from the early spring to the late spring is by observing which flowers are in bloom. Sometimes there are long, dark days and heavy rains, accompanied by the strong wind that shakes the cherry petals from the trees. The new leaves are young and green, too strong to get blown to the ground.

One Saturday in May, I was driving home from eXitSPACE in the rain. When I first left ballet class, the wind and rain was torrential, then by the time I wended my way around the road into Fremont, the rain had slowed to a sprinkle. As I drove up the back side of Queen Anne Hill, it hit me that one day I will take my last ballet class. The time will come, either through age or infirmity, when I can no longer lift my leg to the *Barré*. I think the day when it happens, it really will not stop me from dancing. Even when I am an old woman, I will tap my foot, make a strange rustling sound, and dance in my head.

When I feel the joy and rhythm in the music, I try to form words, but they do not come. As much as I am skilled with words of my own making, my own words are not enough. So my hands make gestures and before I know it, my feet begin to move. Sometimes only I can only hear the music. It is the same as if I am hearing a voice asking me to dance. I dance to the music in my own head. Tremendous freedom comes to me.

My movement is as soft and as delicate as opening my heart to a poem I have written long ago and forgotten. Now I can remember. I remember the steps. In the midst of movement, I find these moments of stillness: a miracle of silence. Now I know why I want to dance. By finding the stillness in the midst of movement, I have earned the privilege of a lifetime—I come to know who I am. Dance lifts me to a place I did not know I could reach, and it is as close to God as I can go. Dance is what, I believe, God can see. As I drove home, I noticed the road was awash with large cherry blossom petals. Then I saw cherry trees on both sides of the road forming a large pink and green canopy. The entire street was covered with pink petals, like soft ballet slippers.

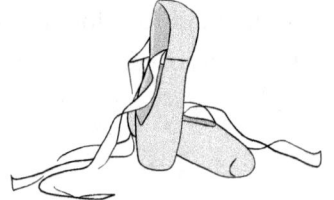

References

"How to Dance Forever: Surviving Against the Odds," by Daniel Nagrin, published 1988 by HarperCollins.

Controlled Moves by BRIAN NEWSOME
Gazette, The (Colorado Springs).Sun Journal June 28 2009
http://www.newbernsj.com/articles/disease-46186-parkinson-willis.html

Learning His Body, Learning to Dance By NEIL GENZLINGER, NYT November 25, 2009   http://www.nytimes.com/2009/11/25/arts/dance/25palsy.html?pagewanted=all

What Don DeLillo's Books Tell Him by Alexandra Alter, WSJ, Jan 30 2010 http://online.wsj.com/article/SB10001424052748704094304575029673526948334.html

Interview with Gelsey Kirkland
Straight from the heart: Gelsey Kirkland looks back ... and ahead
Dance Magazine, Sept, 2005 by Kate Lydon

Darci Kistler Exits the Stage by TONI BENTLEY WSJ, May 28 2010
http://online.wsj.com/article/SB10001424052748704026204575266940794039822.html

Shirley MacLaine on life, showbiz and finding contentment
By Moira Macdonald Seattle Times June 12, 2010
http://seattletimes.nwsource.com/html/movies/2012073537_shirley13.html

American Ballet Theatre Ballet Dictionary
http://www.abt.org/education/dictionary/index.html

Parade magazine   March 21 2010
http://www.parade.com/news/our-towns/2010/0321-dubuque-iowa-dancing-to-defy-expectations.html

What obstacle? Arizona State wrestler brings career to perfect end
By BOB BAUM / The Associated Press I Posted: Friday, March 25, 2011
http://huskerextra.com/mobile/article_1c4ab06b-3803-5025-a7ff-58ba1de4cc13.html

Controlled Moves   Sun Journal June 28 2009
http://www.newbernsj.com/articles/disease-46186-parkinson-willis.html

Quotes attributed to Emilietta Ettlin from Stretch and Strengthen by Judy Alter, Houghton Mifflin Company, 2 Park Street, Boston, MA 02108. A classic.

www.ingramcontent.com/pod-product-compliance
Lightning Source LLC
Chambersburg PA
CBHW050538300426
44113CB00012B/2167